SEASONS & CELEBRATIONS

SEASONS&CELEBRATIONS

A Market-Fresh Cookbook for All Occasions

Recipes and Menus from *Relish*,
America's Most Popular Food Magazine

JILL MELTON, CANDACE FLOYD, AND CHEF JON ASHTON

THE COUNTRYMAN PRESS
Woodstock, Vermont

PUBLISHED BY THE COUNTRYMAN PRESS

P.O. BOX 748 | WOODSTOCK, VERMONT 05091

DISTRIBUTED BY W.W. NORTON & COMPANY, INC.

500 FIFTH AVENUE | NEW YORK, NEW YORK 10110

10 9 8 7 6 5 4 3 2 1

LIBRARY OF CONGRESS CATALOGING-IN-PUBLICATION DATA ARE AVAILABLE

SEASONS & CELEBRATIONS

ISBN: 978-0-88150-837-6

PRINTED IN CHINA BY R.R. DONNELLEY & SONS COMPANY, INC.

COVER IMAGE: LEMON-MARINATED CHICKEN BREASTS, PAGE 79

PHOTOGRAPHS: MARK BOUGHTON PHOTOGRAPHY,
TERESA BLACKBURN, FOOD AND PROP STYLIST;
HIGH COTTON FOOD STYLING & PHOTOGRAPHY
BOOK DESIGN AND ART DIRECTION BY TOM DAVIS

SPINACH AND MUSHROOM PANADE, PAGE 158

ACKNOWLEDGMENTS

JUST AS IT TAKES great ingredients to produce a tasty dish, it takes a great staff to produce a cookbook. Here's our recipe:

Thanks go to *Relish* magazine staples, executive editor Charlie Cox and director of business development Steve Minucci, who cleared the way for this book's creation. Also to Publishing Group of America's president and CEO, Dick Porter, and CFO, Bob Brolund.

Emulsifier Nicki Pendleton Wood pulled it all together, finding just the right recipes, editing them, and preparing the manuscript. For all her hard work, we are very grateful.

The meat and potatoes of any cookbook is recipe testing, and our thanks go to Mary Carter, test kitchen director, who spent hours on end shopping, cooking, and editing recipes.

For the accompaniments to many of the recipes, *Relish* wine columnists Wini Moranville and Charles Smothermon spent countless hours selecting wines to go with the menus. Our thanks go to them for always being willing to answer questions and search for wines that are affordable and widely available.

For the icing on the cake—the beautiful photographs—thanks go to Mark Boughton, photographer; Teresa Blackburn, food and prop stylist; Liz Shenk, assistant food stylist; and Karry Hosford of High Cotton Food Styling and Photography.

We know we eat with our eyes—our plate presentations are due to the hard work of Tom Davis, Publishing Group of America's director of design, who has shared our vision for this book from the beginning.

For the salt and pepper, or seasoning to taste, we are also grateful to Lori Galvin, project editor; Elizabeth Parson, indexer; and Lisa Sacks, our editor at Countryman Press, who offered invaluable advice and expertise that was much appreciated.

INTRODUCTION

WE DAYDREAM about having more parties more often with more people and better food. And while we are perpetually inspired, we are also chronically distracted and pressed for time. Plus, the house is never clean. That said, we think people make the party—and inspire us to cook—whether we've invited two or twenty.

Even though this book is titled *Seasons & Celebrations*, we've included menus for just about any occasion that calls for food, which, in our world, is every occasion. Entertaining can be much more casual and spontaneous than the word implies. Having a soup supper for good friends or a neighborhood cookout with a platter of fajitas is more common today than the cocktail parties of our parents' era. So what you won't find here are fussy, difficult, time-consuming recipes that require taking a sabbatical from work. What you will find are menus for just about every kind of get-together, from a Super Bowl chili buffet to a country couture cookout for Memorial Day. You'll also find recipes for a Fourth of July ice-cream crank, a supper by the fire, and a dinner-and-a-movie party.

But when the occasion calls for pizzazz, there are also recipes for a New Year's Eve lobster dinner, an Easter brunch, variations on Thanksgiving dinner (*serving from 4 to 12*) and a Christmas/Hanukkah dinner party that pulls out all the stops.

Like each issue of *Relish* magazine, *Seasons & Celebrations* features fresh seasonal foods that taste great and require little embellishment. You'll also find tips and menus that make getting food on the table (*or on the sideboard or in the picnic basket*) easier.

So stop fretting over the house (*it will never be totally "done"*), or how good a cook you are, or what your dinnerware looks like. The point of a party is to spend time with friends and family, eating, drinking, and making merry—none of which requires fancy décor or fancy food.

With Relish, the Editors

CONTENTS

WINTER / 01

SPRING / 31

HOLIDAY / 147

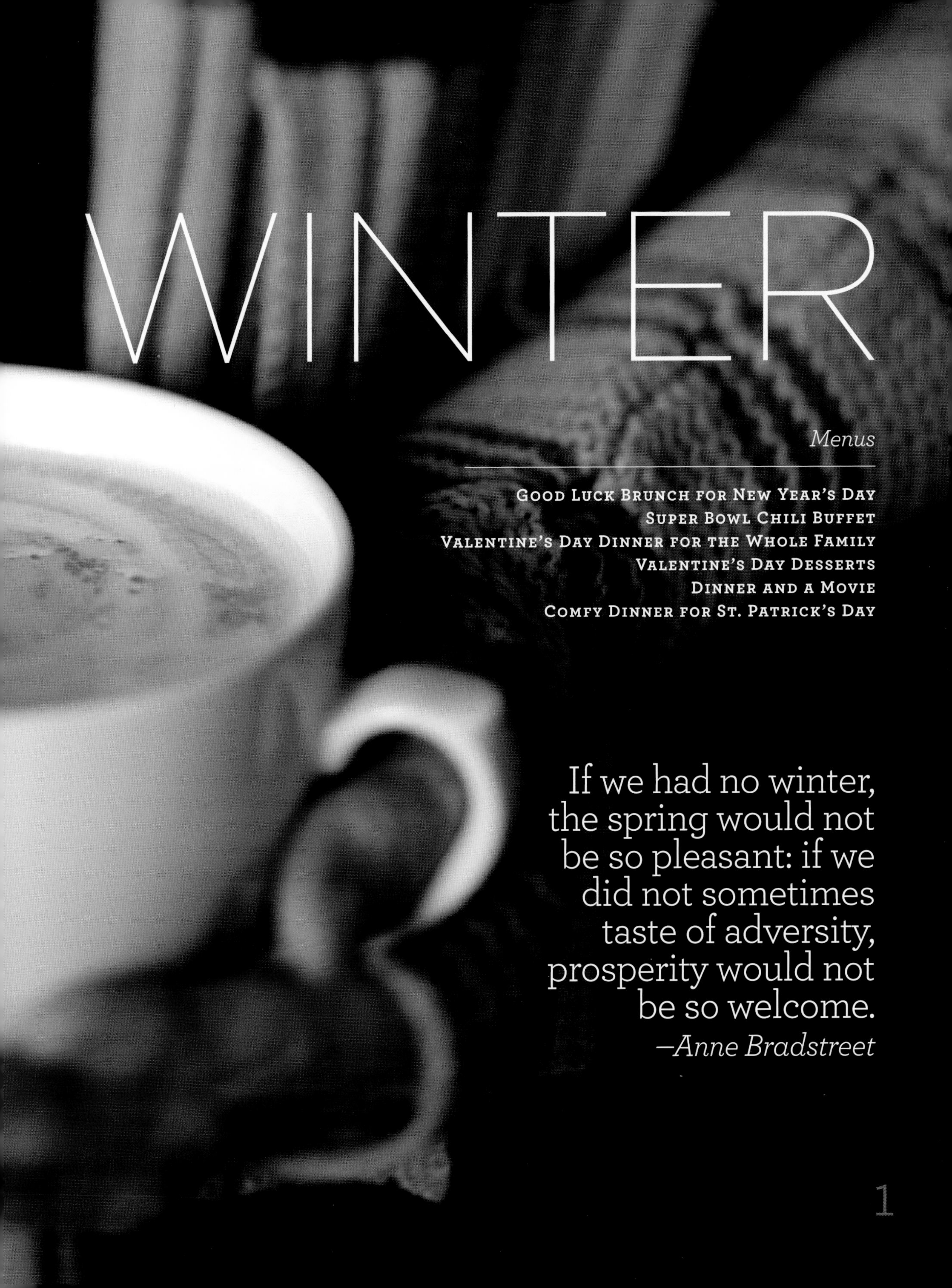

WINTER

Menus

GOOD LUCK BRUNCH FOR NEW YEAR'S DAY
SUPER BOWL CHILI BUFFET
VALENTINE'S DAY DINNER FOR THE WHOLE FAMILY
VALENTINE'S DAY DESSERTS
DINNER AND A MOVIE
COMFY DINNER FOR ST. PATRICK'S DAY

If we had no winter, the spring would not be so pleasant: if we did not sometimes taste of adversity, prosperity would not be so welcome.
—Anne Bradstreet

EAST-WEST BLACK-EYED PEAS

2

Good Luck Brunch for New Year's Day

JANUS, THE ROMAN GOD who gave January its name, was two-faced. He could look forward into the future and backwards into the past. But in planning a New Year's Day brunch, we don't need two faces to make four predictions:

1. Everybody is partied out. They are tired of fancy party food eaten standing up in slinky, glittery, dry-clean-only garments. By New Year's Day, "simple" sounds very good.

2. A New Year's brunch must be easy for the host. Make-ahead dishes are good. Unfussy, easy-to-serve dishes are good. Dishes that are easy on the post-holiday wallet are good too.

3. Fancy? No. Delicious? Yes, of course. Even the most informal drop-in party is still a party. Simply put, the food should taste good and the atmosphere should be comfortable.

4. The food and the occasion should look forward, with hope. As at all beginnings, we may pray for wisdom, courage, and humility. But it doesn't hurt to wish for good luck too.

—Crescent Dragonwagon

> **THE MENU**
>
> EAST-WEST BLACK-EYED PEAS
> COLLARD GREENS SALAD
> CHEESE AND BLACK PEPPER CORNBREAD
> CITRUS GOLDEN RING CAKE

EAST-WEST BLACK-EYED PEAS

Chipotle chile and dark sesame oil give these peas a subtle smokiness. Miso, a fermented soybean paste, is available at natural foods supermarkets (in the refrigerator case) and Asian groceries. In the South, black-eyed peas are traditionally eaten for good luck at New Year's.

3	tablespoons mild vegetable oil
3	garlic cloves
½	dried chipotle chile, broken in half
1	large onion, chopped
2	carrots, chopped
2	celery stalks, chopped
1	red bell pepper, chopped
4	(15-ounce) cans black-eyed peas, drained and rinsed
1 to 2	heaping tablespoons dark or light miso
1	tablespoon dark sesame oil
1	teaspoon salt
	Coarsely ground black pepper

1. Heat vegetable oil in a large, heavy skillet over medium-high heat. Add garlic, chile, and onion; sauté about 8 minutes. Add carrots, celery, and bell pepper; sauté 5 minutes.

2. Remove chipotle and discard. Stir in peas, miso, and sesame oil. Add salt and pepper. Turn heat to medium and continue simmering about 15 minutes, adding a little water, as necessary, to keep peas from sticking. Serves 6.

—Crescent Dragonwagon

PER SERVING: 290 CALORIES, 8G FAT, 0MG CHOL., 15G PROT., 42G CARBS., 8G FIBER, 410MG SODIUM

3

COLLARD GREENS SALAD

Raw collard greens? One bite of these sprightly green ribbons and you'll be a convert. Kale is just as good.

2   (1-pound) bunches collard greens or kale, tough stems removed, leaves washed well
2   tablespoons extra-virgin olive oil
½   teaspoon kosher salt
    Coarsely ground black pepper
    3 to 4 tablespoons freshly squeezed lemon juice

1. In batches, stack collard leaves. Roll them up tightly the long way, making a cigar-shaped roll. Cut across the roll as thinly as possible, making thin ribbons. (*This can be done up to 2 days in advance. Store greens in zip-top plastic bags in refrigerator.*)

2. Place greens in a large salad bowl. Drizzle with oil. Add salt, pepper, and lemon juice. Toss to coat leaves. Serves 8.

—Crescent Dragonwagon

PER SERVING: 70 CALORIES, 4G FAT, 0MG CHOL., 3G PROT., 7G CARBS., 4G FIBER, 140MG SODIUM

CHEESE AND BLACK PEPPER CORNBREAD

This cornbread has a moist crumb and a lovely, crispy-crunchy, cheese-topped crust. Note that the batter will fill the pans only about halfway.

Cooking spray
1 ¼ cups all-purpose flour
1 ¾ cups stone-ground yellow cornmeal
3 tablespoons sugar
4 teaspoons baking powder
½ teaspoon baking soda
1 teaspoon salt
1 teaspoon coarsely ground black pepper
3 eggs
2 ½ cups 2% reduced-fat milk
⅓ cup vegetable oil
1 cup canned creamed corn
1 ¾ cups (8 ounces) shredded sharp Cheddar or Jack cheese
1 tablespoon butter, optional
½ teaspoon kosher salt, optional

1. Preheat oven to 400F. Coat two 8-inch square baking pans with cooking spray.
2. Combine flour, cornmeal, sugar, baking powder, baking soda, salt, and pepper in a medium bowl.
3. Whisk eggs in a medium bowl. Whisk in milk and oil.
4. Pour egg mixture into flour mixture; whisk just until combined. (*Batter will be thinner than typical cornbread batter*). Stir in corn and half of cheese, mixing just until combined. Pour into prepared pans; top with remaining cheese. Bake 35 to 40 minutes, until golden brown. Remove from oven. Spread butter on top and sprinkle with kosher salt if using. Serves 12.
—Crescent Dragonwagon

PER SERVING: 310 CALORIES, 15G FAT, 85MG CHOL., 11G PROT., 33G CARBS., 3G FIBER, 660MG SODIUM

KITCHEN TIP

How to Make a Chiffonade
A chiffonade is a fancy name for a very simple technique—slicing leafy herbs or greens very thinly. Simply stack three or four leaves on a cutting board and roll them up tightly like a cigar. Cut very thin slices as though you were slicing a roll of cookie dough. Presto! You've got a pile of uniformly sized and shaped slivers.

CITRUS GOLDEN RING CAKE

Like the circular wedding ring, a circle speaks of eternity, the circle of life, and the notion that what goes around comes around. This rich, lemony cake, dense and moist, makes anyone who takes a bite feel lucky on the spot. Serve with orange sections and lemon and orange sorbet, if desired.

Cake

	Cooking spray
1 ¾	cups plus 1 tablespoon sugar, divided
3	cups plus 1 tablespoon all-purpose flour, divided
1	cup (2 sticks) butter, softened
3	eggs, at room temperature
½	teaspoon baking soda
½	teaspoon salt
¾	cup buttermilk
¼	cup freshly squeezed orange juice
2	tablespoons freshly squeezed lemon juice
2	tablespoons finely grated lemon rind
1	tablespoon finely grated orange rind

Buttery Citrus Icing

4	tablespoons (½ stick) butter, softened
2	cups sifted powdered sugar
1	tablespoon plus 1 teaspoon finely grated lemon rind
2	teaspoons finely grated orange rind
3	tablespoons freshly squeezed lemon juice
1	tablespoon freshly squeezed orange juice
	Grated orange rind for garnish

1. To prepare cake, preheat oven to 325F. Coat a 10-inch tube pan or 12-cup Bundt pan with cooking spray. Combine 1 tablespoon of sugar and 1 tablespoon of flour. Sprinkle over coated pan, tapping out excess.
2. In a large bowl, beat butter with a mixer at high speed until light and fluffy. Gradually add remaining sugar. Continue beating until well combined. Add eggs, one at a time, beating well after each addition.
3. Sift together remaining flour, baking soda, and salt.
4. Combine buttermilk, orange juice, and lemon juice. Add flour mixture and buttermilk mixture alternately to butter mixture, beginning and ending with flour mixture and beating on low speed. Stir in grated orange and lemon rinds. Pour batter into the prepared pan.
5. Bake 60 to 70 minutes, until the top is golden brown and a wooden pick inserted in the center comes out clean. Let cake cool in the pan on a wire rack 10 minutes. Turn onto a serving plate.
6. To prepare icing, combine butter and sugar using a mixer at medium speed. Add grated lemon and orange rinds. Add lemon and orange juices 1 tablespoon at a time.
7. Pour one-third of icing over cake while still warm. Let cool completely and spread with remaining icing. Sprinkle with orange rind. Serves 16.
—Crescent Dragonwagon

PER SERVING: 340 CALORIES, 16G FAT, 80MG CHOL., 4G PROT., 49G CARBS., 0G FIBER, 160MG SODIUM

Super Bowl Chili Buffet

EVEN HESITANT party-givers can throw a good Super Bowl party. All you need are guests, a big television, chairs, and some chili.

Other than football and food, expectations are modest, so there's little pressure on the host to make special arrangements. A few decorations are nice but not obligatory. And if possible, it's good to offer a football-free room where non-sporty guests can gather.

Our menu is both traditional and easy to make. Our dips are a tasty way to get the party started. And two fresh takes on chili offer good, sturdy Sunday afternoon food meant to satisfy rather than impress, just like the party itself.

THE MENU

CHICKEN CHILI
DRIED CHERRY–TURKEY CHILI
ROASTED RED PEPPER DIP
CREAMY ENCHILADA DIP
SPINACH DIP WITH FETA
SMOKY BLACK BEAN DIP
MOTHER'S SCONES

CHICKEN CHILI

Feel free to experiment with some of the ingredients in this chili—substitute cannellini beans for the garbanzos or pork sausage for the turkey sausage. Kale gives the chili an extra dose of wholesomeness and barley provides fiber. The garnishes are a must.

- 2   tablespoons olive oil
- 1   cup chopped leeks or onion
- 3   garlic cloves, chopped
- 2   teaspoons ground cumin
- 1   teaspoon cumin seed
- 1   pound bulk turkey sausage
- 3   cups chopped cooked chicken
- ⅔   cup pearl barley
- 2   (15-ounce) cans garbanzo beans, drained and rinsed
- 2   teaspoons finely chopped pickled jalapeño chiles
- 6   cups lower-sodium chicken broth
- 4 to 8 cups chopped kale (optional)

Garnishes
Shredded Monterey Jack or Cheddar cheese
Chopped green onions
Sour cream

Heat oil in a Dutch oven over medium heat. Add leeks and garlic; sauté 5 minutes. Add cumin, cumin seed, and sausage. Cook until sausage is browned. Add chicken, barley, beans, jalapeño, broth, and kale, if using. Bring to a boil and simmer until barley is cooked, about 20 minutes. Serve topped with cheese, green onions, and sour cream. Serves 10.
—Jill Melton

PER SERVING: 360 CALORIES, 14G FAT, 100MG CHOL., 30G PROT., 30G CARBS., 7G FIBER, 830MG SODIUM

SIMPLE SOLUTION

Super Bowl High Tea
For those with an aversion to the gridiron, or for those who just want a break from football cheer, try high tea. Instead of touchdowns and conversions, enjoy conversation, perhaps in front of a fire, with hot tea, classic scones, and meat-filled finger sandwiches.

DRIED CHERRY–TURKEY CHILI

This chili is loaded with antioxidants. Garnish with corn tortilla strips, red onion, and avocado.

2	cups lower-sodium chicken broth, divided
4	ounces (¾ cup) dried tart cherries, chopped
1	tablespoon olive oil
1	cup chopped onion
1	tablespoon chopped garlic
2	teaspoons finely chopped jalapeño chile
1	pound ground turkey
1	roasted red bell pepper, chopped
1	tablespoon plus 1 teaspoon chili powder
1 ½	teaspoons ground cumin
1	teaspoon ground coriander
1	teaspoon dried mustard
½	teaspoon dried oregano
2	(14.5-ounce) cans chopped fire-roasted tomatoes, undrained
1	(15-ounce) can black beans, drained and rinsed
¼	cup chopped fresh cilantro

Garnishes

Corn tortilla strips
Chopped red onion
Sliced avocado

1. Heat 1 cup of broth in a saucepan until just simmering. Place cherries in a small bowl. Add hot broth and set aside.
2. Heat olive oil in a large saucepan over medium heat. Add onion; sauté until onion is soft, about 5 minutes. Add garlic and jalapeño; cook 1 minute. Do not brown. Add turkey, stirring to crumble, and cook until it is no longer pink.
3. Add bell pepper, chili powder, cumin, coriander, mustard, and oregano. Turn heat to medium-high and cook, stirring occasionally, about 2 minutes. Add tomatoes and remaining 1 cup broth; bring to a boil. Reduce heat and simmer, uncovered, about 5 minutes.
4. Stir in beans, cilantro, and cherry mixture and cook until thoroughly heated. Serves 8.
—Cherry Marketing Institute

PER SERVING: 230 CALORIES, 6G FAT, 35MG CHOL., 13G PROT., 29G CARBS., 6G FIBER, 660MG SODIUM

WINE PICK
An Argentinean malbec or blend, such as La Posta's Cocina Blend or Gascon Malbec (Mendoza, Argentina) would get along nicely with our Dried Cherry-Turkey Chili.

ROASTED RED PEPPER DIP

Serve with shrimp cocktail,
raw vegetables, crackers, or pita bread.

1	garlic clove
2	red or orange bell peppers, roasted
½	cup toasted pecans
1	tablespoon vinegar
½	cup grated Parmigiano-Reggiano cheese
3	tablespoons extra-virgin olive oil (or enough to make dip creamy)

Pulse garlic in a food processor until chopped. Add remaining ingredients and process until creamy. Serves 7.
—Jill Melton

PER (1/4-CUP) SERVING: 140 CALORIES, 13G FAT, 5MG CHOL., 3G PROT., 3G CARBS., 90MG SODIUM

CREAMY ENCHILADA DIP

This dip tastes like red enchilada sauce and is best served with salty tortilla chips. You can make this dip ahead through step 5 and store it, covered, in the refrigerator up to 1 week. It's also great as a sauce for pasta, shrimp, or chicken.

8	dried mild red chiles (about 2 ounces), such as guajillo or pasilla, seeded and deveined
2	tablespoons canola oil
1	large onion, halved and thinly sliced
2	garlic cloves, minced
1 ½	cups lower-sodium chicken or vegetable broth
1	teaspoon dried oregano
1	teaspoon ground cumin
½	teaspoon salt
½	cup sour cream
1	tablespoon honey

1. Break chiles into large pieces; toast in a large, dry skillet over medium heat, stirring constantly, until fragrant, about 2 minutes. Transfer to a plate.

2. Add oil to the pan, reduce heat, and add onion. Cook, stirring occasionally, until golden, about 10 minutes.

3. Add garlic; cook 20 seconds. Add broth and scrape the pan to loosen browned bits.

4. Stir in toasted chiles, oregano, cumin, and salt; bring to a simmer. Cover, reduce heat, and cook until chiles are very soft, about 15 minutes.

5. Pour mixture into a blender; let cool 15 minutes. Process until smooth. Scrape into a bowl and let cool 10 minutes. Cover with plastic wrap and refrigerate until cold.

6. Just before serving, whisk in sour cream and honey. Serves 8.

—Bruce Weinstein and Mark Scarbrough

PER (1/4-CUP) SERVING: 100 CALORIES, 6G FAT, 10MG CHOL., 3G PROT., 8G CARBS., 1G FIBER, 270MG SODIUM

SPINACH DIP WITH FETA

Originally made with full-fat mayonnaise and dried soup mix, spinach dips have been popular for more than half a century. In this version, lower in fat and salt, a modest amount of feta adds terrific flavor. Serve with table crackers.

¾	cup fat-free sour cream
½	cup 2% reduced-fat cottage cheese
1	(10-ounce) package frozen chopped spinach, excess water squeezed out
2	green onions, white and light green parts, thinly sliced
2	teaspoons lemon juice
¼	teaspoon kosher salt
⅛	teaspoon coarsely ground black pepper
⅓	cup crumbled feta cheese

Place sour cream and cottage cheese in bowl of a food processor; process until smooth. Add spinach, green onions, lemon juice, salt and pepper; process to combine. Add feta and pulse just until combined. Transfer to bowl. Cover and refrigerate at least 1 hour. Makes 2 cups.

—Jean Kressy

PER (1/4-CUP) SERVING: 60 CALORIES, 2G FAT, 10MG CHOL., 4G PROT., 6G CARBS., 1G FIBER, 250MG SODIUM.

SMOKY BLACK BEAN DIP

Serve with corn chips, or for a great sandwich, spread on bread or a wrap with steamed vegetables and salsa.
Note that turtle beans are a little smaller than regular black beans.

12	ounces (about 2 cups) dried black turtle beans or dried black beans
1	garlic clove, chopped
1	tablespoon ground cumin
½	cup peanut butter or almond butter
2	teaspoons salt
½	cup freshly squeezed lime or lemon juice
1	tablespoon chopped chipotle chile in adobo sauce
2	tablespoons extra-virgin olive oil
¼	cup water
1 to 2	cups grape tomato halves

1. Place beans in a large Dutch oven. Add enough water to cover beans by 2 inches. Bring to a boil. Remove from heat and let stand, covered, 1 hour. Drain beans and return to pot. Cover with cold water and bring to a boil. Lower heat to a simmer, cover, and cook until tender but not mushy, 45 minutes to 1 hour. Drain beans and discard cooking water.
2. Place garlic in a small bowl, cover, and microwave on high 30 seconds.
3. Place beans in a food processor with garlic, cumin, peanut butter, salt, lime juice, chile, oil, and water. Process until smooth, adding more water, as necessary, to purée completely. Scrape into a bowl. Cover and let stand 30 minutes to 1 hour for flavors to blend. Arrange tomato halves on top, cut-side down. Serves 20.
—Nancy Krcek Allen

PER (1/2-CUP) SERVING: 230 CALORIES, 10G FAT, 0MG CHOL., 11G PROT., 26G CARBS., 10G FIBER, 525MG SODIUM

MOTHER'S SCONES

We love this scone recipe, from Mother's Bistro in Portland, Oregon. It can support lots of variations — try adding your favorite spices, fresh fruit, dried fruit, citrus zests, or flavor extracts. Or make indentations in the tops of the scones and fill with jam before baking.

Scones
2 ¼	cups all-purpose flour
⅓	cup granulated sugar
1	tablespoon baking powder
11	tablespoons (1 stick plus 3 tablespoons) cold unsalted butter, cut into small pieces
1	cup cold heavy cream

Vanilla Icing
1	cup powdered sugar
¼	teaspoon vanilla extract
1 ½	tablespoons water

1. To prepare scones, preheat oven to 375F.

2. Whisk together flour, granulated sugar, and baking powder in a large bowl until well combined.

3. Using a pastry blender or your hands, blend butter into dry ingredients until mixture is the consistency of coarse meal.

4. Add cream; stir just until blended.

5. Turn out onto a lightly floured surface and knead lightly until smooth dough forms. Pat into a square about 1 inch thick. Cut dough into 16 triangles (*cut into 4 squares first, then cut each square into fourths diagonally*). Arrange 1 inch apart on a parchment-lined baking sheet.

6. Bake 15 to 20 minutes, until lightly browned. Transfer to a wire rack set over a baking sheet to cool while preparing icing.

7. To prepare icing, mix powdered sugar and vanilla extract in a small bowl. Add water, a little at a time, until thin enough to drizzle over scones.

8. Dip end of a whisk into icing, then wave over warm scones. Yield: 16 scones.

—Mother's Bistro

PER SCONE (WITH ICING): 220 CALORIES, 13G FAT, 40MG CHOL., 2G PROT., 24G CARBS., 0G FIBER, 110MG SODIUM

13

Valentine's Day Dinner for the Whole Family

CONVENTIONAL WISDOM is that parents go out—or stay home alone—on Valentine's Day. But the realities are that Valentine's Day often falls on a school night; restaurant reservations fill before we've had a chance to pick up the phone; and even if we did secure a reservation, the babysitter probably has her own Valentine's planned. Enter Valentine's Day for the entire family.

This dinner starring your favorite steak with Cilantro Chimichurri brings that special restaurant entrée to your table. If you're on a burger budget, make it a special one with Two-Cheese Basil Burgers. Everyone will love Microwaved Mashed Potatoes, especially the cook, who can skip the chopping and boiling with this easy technique. Fresh spinach is a reminder of spring just around the corner.

And another bit of wisdom—buy chocolates for dessert.

THE MENU

TWO-CHEESE BASIL BURGERS **or** CILANTRO CHIMICHURRI FOR GRILLED STEAK GRILLED PORTOBELLO MUSHROOM SALAD STIR-FRIED SPINACH

TWO-CHEESE BASIL BURGERS

Cooking spray
1 ½ pounds ground chuck
¼ cup chopped fresh basil
2 garlic cloves, minced
½ teaspoon kosher salt
Coarsely ground black pepper
⅓ cup red wine
4 tablespoons Boursin cheese
4 (1-ounce) slices mozzarella cheese
Arugula
4 slices tomato
Balsamic vinegar
4 ciabatta or focaccia buns

1. Preheat grill and coat the grill rack with cooking spray.
2. Combine beef, basil, garlic, salt, pepper, and wine. Form into 4 patties. Make an indentation in center of each burger to hold cheeses.
3. Grill burgers, indentation-side down, 5 minutes; turn. Top with boursin and mozzarella cheese. Grill 5 minutes more. Place arugula on bottom halves of buns. Top with burger and tomato. Drizzle with balsamic vinegar and cover with buns. Serves 4.
—Relish Chef Jon Ashton

PER SERVING: 390 CALORIES, 17G FAT, 90MG CHOL., 33G PROT., 25G CARBS., 1G FIBER, 600MG SODIUM

WINE PICK
Pair a juicy steak with Mumm Napa Reserve Brut Sparkling Wine, a sparkler that includes 60 percent Pinot Noir. This food-friendly wine can take you from appetizer through dessert.

CILANTRO CHIMICHURRI FOR GRILLED STEAK

Chimichurri is similar to pesto and has as many variations as there are cooks. This version incorporates cilantro and resembles the chimichurri most often found in Central America. Use it as a marinade, basting sauce, or condiment for grilled steak or chicken.

6	garlic cloves
1	cup fresh cilantro
1	cup fresh flat-leaf parsley
½	cup chopped onion
2	tablespoons white wine vinegar
½	teaspoon dried oregano
½	teaspoon crushed red pepper
½	cup extra-virgin olive oil
½	teaspoon salt
	Coarsely ground black pepper

1. Place garlic in a food processor; pulse until finely chopped. Add cilantro, parsley, onion, vinegar, oregano, and crushed red pepper.

2. Add olive oil in a thin stream and process until smooth. Add salt and pepper. The dip can be refrigerated, covered, up to 1 week. Serve with steak or chicken. Serves 8.

—Sandra Gutierrez

PER (1/4-CUP) SERVING: 140 CALORIES, 14G FAT, 0MG CHOL., 1G PROT., 2G CARBS., 1G FIBER, 150MG SODIUM

KITCHEN TIP

Microwave Mashed Potatoes
Place potatoes in a microwave-safe dish and cover. (If using plastic wrap, poke a small hole in the plastic.) Microwave on high 8 minutes or until potatoes are thoroughly cooked. Transfer potatoes to a large bowl. Add milk, butter, salt, and pepper. Mash with a potato masher to desired consistency.

GRILLED PORTOBELLO MUSHROOM SALAD

Cooking spray
¼ cup olive oil
4 tablespoons red wine vinegar
2 teaspoons country-style Dijon mustard
⅛ teaspoon salt
4 large portobello mushroom caps
4 ounces goat cheese, room temperature
1 small bunch baby arugula, stems trimmed
16 grape tomatoes, cut into halves

1. Preheat grill and coat the grill rack with cooking spray (*or preheat broiler*).
2. Whisk together oil, vinegar, mustard, and salt.
3. Place mushroom caps on a plate, gill-side down, and drizzle with half of vinaigrette. Grill or broil mushrooms about 5 minutes.
3. Turn caps over and top with goat cheese. Return to grill or oven. Cook until cheese melts slightly.
4. In a medium bowl, toss arugula with remaining vinaigrette and tomatoes. Divide among four plates; top each with a warm, cheese-topped mushroom. Serves 4.
—Rosell Bocchieri

PER SERVING: 290 CALORIES, 23G FAT, 20MG CHOL., 10G PROT., 10G CARBS., 3G FIBER, 300MG SODIUM

STIR-FRIED SPINACH
This recipe also works well in an Asian-themed menu as a complement to steamed whole fish or poached chicken. Depending on the size of your wok or skillet, you may need to make this in two batches.

1 tablespoon peanut oil
5 garlic cloves, finely chopped
1 teaspoon salt
2 (9-ounce) bags spinach leaves, washed and trimmed (about 16 cups loosely packed)
1 teaspoon sugar

1. Heat a wok or large skillet over high heat. Add peanut oil; swirl to coat the bottom. When very hot and slightly smoking, add chopped garlic and salt. Stir-fry about 15 seconds.
2. Add spinach. Stir-fry until leaves are thoroughly coated with oil and spinach is wilted, about 2 minutes.
3. Add sugar and stir-fry 4 minutes. Transfer to a warm plate. Pour off excess liquid. Serves 4.
—Christina Eng

PER SERVING: 90 CALORIES, 3.5G FAT, 0MG CHOL., 3G PROT., 15G CARBS., 6G FIBER, 780MG SODIUM

Valentine's Day Desserts

AS THE STORY GOES, a guy found a bottle on the ocean. He opened it and out popped a genie, who was so grateful that she offered to grant him three wishes. The guy wished for a million dollars and poof! There was a million dollars. Then he wished for a convertible and poof! There was a convertible. Then he wished he could be irresistible to all women and poof! He turned into a box of chocolates.

The genie knew that for many women, chocolate is almost as necessary as water. So just in time for Valentine's Day, a collection of chocolaty desserts for you and your sweetie. More than you could wish for.

THE MENU

BITTERSWEET CHOCOLATE RUM TORTE
FLOURLESS CHOCOLATE CAKE
WITH STRAWBERRIES AND CREAM
MAYAN HOT CHOCOLATE
NO-COOK CHOCOLATE SILK TARTS
CHOCOLATE ESPRESSO SOUFFLÉ

BITTERSWEET CHOCOLATE RUM TORTE

This warm, creamy torte is a chocolate lover's dream. It is made very quickly and can be popped into the oven just before you sit down to dinner. Make the vanilla custard sauce ahead and chill until serving.

Vanilla Custard Sauce
- 1 ½ cups half-and-half
- 3 egg yolks, lightly beaten
- ½ cup sugar
- ⅛ teaspoon salt
- 2 teaspoons vanilla extractt

Torte
- Cooking spray
- 4 ounces semisweet or bittersweet chocolate
- 3 tablespoons dark rum
- 4 tablespoons (½ stick) unsalted butter, softened
- ¾ cup sugar, divided
- 4 eggs, separated
- 2 tablespoons Dutch-processed cocoa
- ⅛ teaspoon salt

1. To prepare custard sauce, whisk together half-and-half, egg yolks, sugar, and salt in a heavy saucepan. Cook over medium heat, stirring frequently, until thickened. Let cool slightly and stir in vanilla. Place plastic wrap on surface; chill several hours or overnight.

2. Preheat oven to 300F. Coat bottom and sides of an 8-inch springform pan with cooking spray.

3. To prepare torte, combine chocolate and rum in a bowl set over simmering water. Stir until chocolate melts. (*Or place bowl in microwave and microwave on medium 30 seconds. Stir. Repeat until chocolate melts.*)

4. Beat butter with a mixer on medium speed until smooth. Gradually add ½ cup of sugar and beat until smooth and fluffy, 2 to 3 minutes. Add egg yolks and beat 1 minute. On low speed, beat in chocolate mixture (*which may still be warm*) until thoroughly combined. Add cocoa and beat until incorporated.

5. Beat egg whites with salt in a clean bowl with clean, dry beaters until soft peaks form. Gradually beat in remaining sugar, 1 tablespoon at a time, until stiff peaks form.

17

BITTERSWEET CHOCOLATE RUM TORTE

6. Gently fold one-quarter of egg whites into chocolate mixture; gently fold in remaining egg whites. Spoon batter into the prepared pan.

7. Bake 40 to 50 minutes. The torte will rise to the top of the pan during baking but will sink dramatically as it cools. Let cool completely.

8. Remove the side of the springform pan. Cut torte with a sharp knife. Serve with custard sauce. Serves 8. *VARIATION: To make a coffee-flavored torte, melt chocolate with 3 tablespoons Kahlúa or strong brewed coffee instead of rum.*

—Greg Patent

PER SERVING: 290 CALORIES, 18G FAT, 110MG CHOL., 4G PROT., 35G CARBS., 0G FIBER, 95MG SODIUM

FLOURLESS CHOCOLATE CAKE WITH STRAWBERRIES AND CREAM
To grind almonds, place them in the bowl of a food processor and pulse until fine.

Cooking spray
2 tablespoons unsweetened cocoa
8 ounces semisweet chocolate
½ cup (1 stick) unsalted butter
1 cup plus 2 tablespoons sugar, divided
1 cup ground almonds
4 eggs, separated
1 cup cold heavy cream
1 teaspoon vanilla extract
2 cups whole strawberries, hulled

1. Preheat oven to 350F. Coat a 9-inch springform pan with cooking spray and cocoa; shake off excess cocoa.

2. Melt chocolate in a bowl set over simmering water; stir until chocolate melts. (*Or place bowl in microwave and microwave on medium 30 seconds. Stir. Repeat until chocolate melts.*)

3. Place butter in large bowl; beat with a mixer on medium speed until smooth. Add 1 cup sugar; beat until creamy. Add ground almonds, chocolate, and egg yolks; beat until thoroughly combined.

4. In a large, clean bowl, using clean, dry beaters, beat egg whites at high speed until soft peaks form (*do not overbeat*). Stir one-third of egg whites into chocolate mixture; gently fold in remaining egg whites.

5. Scrape batter into the prepared pan. Bake 35 to 40 minutes or until a wooden pick inserted in center comes out almost clean. Let cool 30 minutes in the pan on a wire rack. Release the sides of the pan and slide onto a serving plate.

6. Combine cream, vanilla, and 2 tablespoons sugar in a medium bowl and beat until soft peaks form. Top cake with whipped cream and strawberries. Serves 12.

—Marge Perry

PER SERVING: 330 CALORIES, 24G FAT, 45G CHOL., 4G PROT., 30G CARBS., 3G FIBER, 10MG SODIUM

KITCHEN TIP

Butternut Squash
Frozen, cubed butternut squash is a handy ingredient. In addition to imparting a sweet flavor and creamy texture to our Mayan Hot Chocolate, frozen butternut squash can be used in the following ways:

- Toss it with short pasta, sausage, and Parmigiano-Reggiano cheese.
- Add it to risotto.
- Purée or mash it with aged Cheddar cheese for an alternative to mashed potatoes.
- Include it as a topping for white pizza.

MAYAN HOT CHOCOLATE

1	small butternut squash (or ⅔ cup squash pulp)
2 ½	cups 1% low-fat milk, divided
6	ounces semisweet chocolate
½	teaspoon ground cinnamon
	Large pinch ground nutmeg
	Large pinch ground cardamom

1. Preheat oven to 375F.
2. Cut squash into halves; place halves, cut-sides down, in a roasting pan. Add water to pan to a depth of 1 inch. Bake 30 minutes or until squash is tender. Discard seeds and scoop out enough pulp to measure ⅔ cup. Purée squash with ½ cup of milk in a food processor until smooth.
3. Mix remaining 2 cups milk, chocolate, and spices in a large saucepan or the top of a double boiler over simmering water. Cook until chocolate melts, stirring constantly. Remove from heat and whisk in puréed squash. Return to heat and cook until thoroughly heated. Serves 4.
—Chef Jesus Gonzalez

PER SERVING: 300 CALORIES, 14G FAT, 10MG CHOL., 9G PROT., 39G CARBS., 4G FIBER, 80MG SODIUM

No-Cook Chocolate Silk Tarts

You'd never know tofu is in these creamy tarts. Be sure to use the custard-like silken tofu packaged in vacuum-sealed boxes.

7	ounces semisweet chocolate
1	cup sugar
⅓	cup unsweetened cocoa
⅔	cup low-fat sour cream
1	(12-ounce) box soft silken tofu
1	tablespoon vanilla extract
⅓	cup egg substitute
⅛	teaspoon salt
12	(3-inch) graham cracker tart shells
	Whipped cream (optional)
	Bittersweet chocolate curls (optional)

1. Melt chocolate in a bowl set over simmering water; stir until chocolate melts. (*Or place bowl in microwave and microwave on medium 30 seconds. Stir. Repeat until chocolate melts.*) Let cool slightly.
2. Combine chocolate, sugar, cocoa, sour cream, tofu, vanilla, egg substitute, and salt in a food processor. Pulse until completely smooth, pausing to scrape down sides of processor. Divide filling among tart shells.
3. Cover with waxed paper, then cover tightly with plastic wrap. Chill at least 4 hours, but preferably overnight.
4. Top with whipped cream and chocolate curls, if using. Serves 12.
—Crescent Dragonwagon

PER SERVING: 280 CALORIES, 12G FAT, 5MG CHOL., 5G PROT., 41G CARBS., 1G FIBER, 180MG SODIUM

Chocolate Espresso Soufflé

If you want your soufflé to rise above the dish, use a 4-cup soufflé dish (as in the photo) with a collar. Make a collar by wrapping a strip of buttered parchment paper around the outside of the dish and securing it with a string. The collar should extend 3 or 4 inches above the pan's edge. Serve this soufflé with vanilla ice cream or frozen yogurt.

	Butter for coating the baking dish
½	cup sugar, divided
3	tablespoons brewed espresso or very strong brewed coffee
5	ounces bittersweet chocolate, chopped
4	egg yolks
6	egg whites

1. Preheat oven to 400F. Butter a 2-quart soufflé dish or six 8-ounce ramekins and sprinkle with ¼ of cup sugar.
2. Combine espresso and chocolate in a microwave-safe bowl. Microwave on medium about 30 seconds. Stir and repeat until chocolate melts. Let cool briefly.
3. Whisk egg yolks into chocolate mixture.
4. Beat egg whites in a clean bowl with clean, dry beaters until frothy. Gradually add remaining ¼ cup sugar, beating until soft peaks form.
5. Stir about 1 cup egg white mixture into chocolate mixture; fold in remaining egg white mixture.
6. Spoon into the prepared dish. Place on a baking sheet and bake 30 to 40 minutes for a soufflé dish or 20 to 25 minutes for ramekins until soufflé rises. Serve immediately. Serves 6.
—Tracy Ceurvels

PER SERVING: 210 CALORIES, 13G FAT, 140MG CHOL., 7G PROT., 24G CARBS., 2G FIBER, 65MG SODIUM

Dinner and a Movie

GAB, GIRLFRIENDS, GOOD GRUB, and a movie—what could be better?

It's nowhere near the investment of a book club and it's a lot more fun. "It" is a movie group—friends who gather each month for dinner and a movie.

The host chooses the movie and makes the meal. The meals can be elaborate—sometimes even matching the theme of the movie. Hearty beefy borscht might accompany *The Russians Are Coming*, or pounded "chick" (chicken breasts) might take center stage for *Million Dollar Baby*.

But then, the food really isn't the point. Come to think of it, neither is the movie. It's about the friendship. The good thing is there are no rules, except to show up … preferably hungry.

THE MENU

WINTER MINESTRONE
CRUNCHY CALIFORNIA SUNSHINE SALAD
QUICK CARAMEL BANANA CORNBREAD PUDDING

Winter Minestrone

You can use nearly any vegetable lingering in your fridge to make this soup (although we might skip broccoli and cauliflower). It's great with a can of white beans thrown in too. The hearty kale stands up to the wheat berries, but you can use almost any green. You also can use barley in place of the wheat berries. Look for wheat berries in the grains section of the supermarket.

1	tablespoon olive oil
4	green onions, chopped
½	red or white onion, chopped
1	celery stalk, chopped
3	large carrots, chopped
4	ounces finely chopped sliced deli ham
3	cups water
3	cups lower-sodium chicken broth
1	cup wheat berries, rinsed
1	Parmigiano-Reggiano cheese rind (optional)
2	bay leaves
½	teaspoon salt
	Coarsely ground black pepper
1	(14.5-ounce) can diced tomatoes with basil, undrained
1	(1-pound) bag kale, chopped
4	toasted pita breads, cut into halves

Heat oil in a large saucepan or Dutch oven. Add onions, celery, carrots, and ham. Sauté 10 minutes. Add water and next 6 ingredients (*water through pepper*). Bring to a boil; reduce heat and simmer, covered, until wheat berries are tender, about 30 minutes. Stir in tomatoes and kale; cook until thoroughly heated. (*The longer the cheese rind remains in the soup, the more intense the flavor becomes.*) Serve with toasted pita bread. Serves 8.
—Jill Melton

PER (2-CUP) SERVING: 260 CALORIES, 3G FAT, 10MG CHOL., 12G PROT., 47G CARBS., 6G FIBER, 880MG SODIUM

Parmigiano-Reggiano

Like Champagne (which must be produced in the Champagne region of France to earn the name), cheese labeled Parmigiano-Reggiano must be made in government-designated sections of northern Italy under very specific rules—only from morning and evening milk from cows fed special grasses. Once you have tasted true Parmigiano-Reggiano, you'll be hooked. To know if you have the real thing, look for the pin-dot label on the rind that spells out Parmigiano-Reggiano.

Here are some new ways to use Parmigiano-Reggiano:

• Save the rinds to flavor soups. Toss in and let stew at least 30 minutes.
• Add 2 tablespoons Parmigiano-Reggiano cheese to savory pie, tart, and pizza crusts.
• Use in macaroni and cheese along with cream cheese, sharp Cheddar, and Gruyère.

CRUNCHY CALIFORNIA SUNSHINE SALAD

Make the dressing a few hours ahead and chill. You'll use only about half of the dressing.
Refrigerate remaining dressing up to 1 week.

Dressing
8 ounces cream cheese, softened
2 teaspoons grated orange rind
1 cup freshly squeezed orange juice (about 2 medium oranges)
1 tablespoon honey
1 tablespoon Dijon mustard
1 teaspoon salt

Salad
2 heads baby romaine lettuce, torn into bite-sized pieces
2 navel oranges, peeled and segmented
2 (4-ounce) packages bean sprouts
⅓ cup chopped jicama
⅓ cup golden raisins
⅓ cup dried sour cherries or cranberries
⅓ cup sunflower seed kernels

1. To prepare dressing: combine all ingredients in a blender and process until smooth and creamy. Chill.
2. To prepare salad, place lettuce in a large salad bowl. Cut each orange segment into halves and add to lettuce. Add bean sprouts, jicama, raisins, cherries, and sunflower seed kernels. When ready to serve, pour about half the chilled dressing over salad and toss. Serves 8.
—Michaela Rosenthal

PER SERVING: 150 CALORIES, 8G FAT, 15MG CHOL., 4G PROT., 16G CARBS., 2G FIBER, 240MG SODIUM

QUICK CARAMEL BANANA CORNBREAD PUDDING

Corn muffins or leftover cornbread make this decadent dessert—reminiscent of Bananas Foster—a snap.
Be sure to crumble the muffins into large chunks. Serve warm with vanilla ice cream.

1 (8-ounce) package corn muffin mix
Butter for coating baking dish
3 bananas, sliced
¾ cup dark brown sugar, divided
3 cups 2% reduced-fat milk
4 eggs
½ teaspoon ground ginger
½ teaspoon ground cinnamon
¼ cup caramel sauce or topping

1. Prepare corn muffins according to package instructions. Let cool. Crumble 4 muffins into large chunks. (*Reserve remaining muffins for another use.*)
2. Preheat oven to 325F. Lightly butter a 2-quart or 8-inch-square ceramic baking dish or six 8-ounce ramekins.
3. Arrange banana slices in the dish. Top with ¼ cup of brown sugar and chunks of corn muffins. Combine milk, eggs, remaining ½ cup brown sugar, ginger, and cinnamon; whisk to blend. Pour over crumbled muffins. Bake 50 minutes or until pudding is barely set. Drizzle with caramel sauce and serve warm. Serves 6.
—Jill Melton

PER SERVING: 520 CALORIES, 12G FAT, 170MG CHOL., 14G PROT., 92G CARBS., 4G FIBER, 550MG SODIUM

Comfy Dinner for St. Patrick's Day

HOW, IN THE NAME of all things authentic and Irish, did the green in St. Patrick's Day celebrations become all about green food coloring? From green beer to green bagels, a few drops of green coloring does not an Irish dish make.

The green of the Emerald Isle is not from a bottle, but from the verdant grass covering this ancient, sea-surrounded, hilly land. The terrain gives Irish cheeses an underlying sweetness.

And as for green beer: If you're talking authentic and Irish, think ale and think red, not green. Medium-bodied, malty, a bit fruity and a distinct golden-red.

Put together in a new way, Irish ingredients become a fresh menu of corned beef and cabbage salad, a glorious soup, thick and creamy, combining Irish cheeses, ale and potatoes, and to top it all off, Irish Kona coffee.

—*Crescent Dragonwagon*

CORNED BEEF AND CABBAGE SALAD

We're always looking for something new to do with corned beef. Here we rethink the traditional braise by turning it into a hearty main-dish salad. You'll have some of the dressing left over. Refrigerate up to 1 week.

Mustard-Molasses Vinaigrette
- ½   cup Dijon mustard
- ½   cup whole grain mustard
- ½   cup brown sugar
- 1   tablespoon molasses
- ¼   cup cider vinegar
- 1   garlic clove, crushed
- 1   teaspoon crushed red pepper

Salad
- 1   pound corned beef, fat trimmed, cut into 3-inch lengths across grain and shredded
- 2   cups cooked Yukon gold potatoes, peeled and cut into bite-sized pieces
- 1   cup halved green beans or haricots verts, blanched
- 1   cup sliced green cabbage
- 2   tablespoons mayonnaise
- 1   tablespoon chopped chives

1. To prepare vinaigrette, whisk together all the ingredients. Chill.
2. To prepare salad, combine all ingredients, except chives, in a large bowl.
3. Add ⅓ cup vinaigrette to the salad. (*You'll have some dressing left over.*) Toss gently. Garnish with chives. Serves 6.
—Vincent Nattress, Napa Valley Mustard Festival

PER SERVING: 190 CALORIES, 6G FAT, 40MG CHOL., 15G PROT., 17G CARBS., 2G FIBER, 730MG SODIUM

Irish Potato Soup with Cheese and Red Ale

Use all leeks or all onions instead of a combination of the two if you like. The potatoes may be peeled or unpeeled and you may use a more readily available beer or ale. Serve with a spinach salad and whole grain toast or crisp baguette slices instead of the Corned Beef and Cabbage Salad for a lighter meal.

4	tablespoons (½ stick) butter, divided
2	cups chopped onion
2	leeks, sliced
¾	cup sliced celery (about 3 stalks)
8	Yukon gold potatoes, peeled and coarsely chopped (about 2 ¾ pounds)
1	(12-ounce) bottle Irish red ale
4	cups lower-sodium chicken or vegetable broth
½	teaspoon salt
	Coarsely ground pepper to taste
3	tablespoons all-purpose flour
4	cups whole or 2% reduced-fat milk
1 ¾	cups (7 ounces) grated Kerrygold Dubliner cheese

Garnishes (optional)
Finely minced parsley
Crumbled blue cheese
Bacon, cooked until crisp and crumbled

1. Melt 2 tablespoons of butter in a 6- to 8-quart stockpot. Add onion, leeks, and celery and stir. Cook over medium heat about 10 minutes.
2. Add potatoes, ale, broth, salt, and pepper. Bring to a boil; simmer, covered, over low heat until potatoes are tender, about 45 minutes.
3. Melt remaining 2 tablespoons butter in a medium saucepan; gradually whisk in flour. Cook 3 minutes on medium-low heat, stirring constantly. Gradually stir in milk, whisking until hot and thickened. Add cheese; stir until melted.
4. Stir cheese mixture into potato mixture until combined. Cook over very low heat 10 minutes.
5. Ladle into soup bowls and sprinkle with parsley, blue cheese, and bacon, if using. Serves 8.
NOTE: If you can't find Kerrygold Dubliner, substitute 4 ounces Gruyère combined with 4 ounces of medium sharp white Cheddar.
—Crescent Dragonwagon

PER (1 3/4-CUP) SERVING: 420 CALORIES, 18G FAT, 55MG CHOL., 16G PROT., 49G CARBS., 4G FIBER, 640MG SODIUM

IRISH KONA COFFEE

- 4   cups strong brewed Kona coffee
- ¼   cup plus 2 tablespoons sugar, divided
- ½   cup plus 2 tablespoons Irish whiskey, divided
- 1   cup cold heavy cream

1. Place coffee in a saucepan with ¼ cup of sugar. Add ½ cup of Irish whiskey and heat thoroughly, but do not boil.

2. Beat cream with a mixer on medium-high speed until it holds soft peaks. Beat in remaining 2 tablespoons sugar and remaining 2 tablespoons Irish whiskey.

3. Pour coffee into mugs and spoon flavored cream on top. Serves 4.

—Martin Booe

PER SERVING: 340 CALORIES, 22G FAT, 80MG CHOL., 2G PROT., 15G CARBS., 0G FIBER, 30MG SODIUM

SIMPLE SOLUTION

Beer and Cheese Pairings
With the growing number of brews on the market, selecting beer can be just as complex as choosing a wine. Try these beer-and-cheese matches for your next get-together.
—*Lauren Shockey*

TYPE OF CHEESE	BEER TO PAIR	BRAND
Emmental	Bock beer	SHINER BOCK
Cheddar	Nut brown ale	NEWCASTLE
Brie or goat cheese	Crisp, floral pilsner	PILSNER URQUELL
Gruyère	Wheat beer	HOEGAARDEN
Kaseri or sheep's milk feta	Highly carbonated wheat beer	BLUE MOON
Parmigiano-Reggiano	Smooth porter	MICHELOB PORTER
Mozzarella	India pale ale	SIERRA NEVADA PALE ALE
Roquefort	Yeasty Trappist ale	CHIMAY BLEUE
Cheez Whiz	Amber lager	SAMUEL ADAMS BOSTON LAGER
American	Medium-hop pilsner	STELLA ARTOIS

SPRING

Menus

PASSOVER SUPPER
EASTER BRUNCH
CINCO DE MAYO CELEBRATION
MOTHER'S DAY DINNER
COUNTRY COUTURE COOKOUT FOR MEMORIAL DAY

Spring is nature's way of saying, "Let's party!"–*Robin Williams*

30

Passover Supper

PASSOVER IS A HOLIDAY that revolves around food, which may help explain why it is celebrated by more Jews than any other holiday.

The eight-day religious observance begins with the seder dinner, during which the exodus story is remembered and retold through symbolic foods. Matzo, or unleavened bread, takes center stage, symbolizing the hasty flight of the Jews from enslavement in Egypt. Jewish law dating back to ancient times mandates that no grain or leavened product be eaten for the duration of the holiday—just matzo. Our menu celebrates with apple fritters made with matzo and a farfel kugel with artichokes and shiitake mushrooms that can be served year-round.

Cherished traditions and flavors get an overhaul on the rest of our menu. Roasted Cornish hens are baked in a marinade with both Middle Eastern and Cuban flavors. The red wine, raisins, and walnuts that traditionally flavor haroset turn up in an eggplant caponata salad. It's a Passover meal for the new American table.

> **THE MENU**
>
> **CORNISH HENS WITH ZA'ATAR MOJO**
> **EGGPLANT CAPONATA**
> **MUSHROOM, ARTICHOKE, AND ONION MATZO KUGEL**
> **APPLE FRITTERS**

CORNISH HENS WITH ZA'ATAR MOJO

We've added the dried herb called za'atar (see page 37) to our mojo, which is a Cuban marinade traditionally containing oil, garlic, and sour oranges. Look for za'atar and sumac in Middle Eastern markets.

Za'atar Mojo

- ¼ cup vegetable oil
- ¼ cup olive oil
- 1 cup whole garlic cloves, peeled and thinly sliced (about 3 heads)
- 1 jalapeño chile, seeded and very thinly sliced
- 1 tablespoon za'atar (optional)
- 1½ teaspoons sumac (a Middle Eastern spice)
- ¾ cup freshly squeezed lemon juice
- ¼ cup chopped parsley
- ¼ teaspoon salt
- ¼ teaspoon coarsely ground black pepper
- 4 small Cornish game hens

1. To prepare mojo, heat oils in a medium saucepan over high heat for 2 minutes. Add garlic, gently shaking the pan until garlic begins to turn golden. Remove from heat and add jalapeño, za'atar, and sumac. Add lemon juice, parsley, salt, and pepper. Let cool.
2. Combine hens and mojo in a large zip-top plastic bag. Place in refrigerator; marinate at least 12 but no more than 24 hours. Place hens, breast-side up, and marinade in a roasting pan or baking dish; let stand at room temperature 15 minutes before roasting.
3. Preheat oven to 375F.
4. Roast hens 1 hour or until skin is golden, juices run clear, and the internal temperature of the thigh reaches 180F, basting occasionally with marinade. Serve with pan juices. Serves 4.
—Chef Michelle Bernstein

PER SERVING: 430 CALORIES, 22G FAT, 215MG CHOL., 49G PROT., 62G CARBS., 0G FIBER, 240 MG SODIUM

EGGPLANT CAPONATA

Eggplant Caponata

This all-purpose dish, with its bright, bold flavors, works well as an appetizer with matzo crackers or as a relish for grilled chicken or fish.

¼ cup olive oil
2 large eggplants (about 1 pound each), cut into ½-inch cubes
1 large onion, chopped
1 (14.5-ounce) can diced tomatoes, drained
½ cup kalamata olives, pitted and cut into halves
½ cup red wine
¼ cup coarsely chopped walnuts
¼ cup golden raisins
2 tablespoons tomato paste
2 tablespoons balsamic vinegar
1 tablespoon capers
¼ teaspoon salt
¼ teaspoon coarsely ground black pepper
2 tablespoons chopped fresh parsley

WINE PICKS
Labeled "Kosher for Passover," Yarden 2007 Odem Organic Vineyard Chardonnay from Israel offers orchard fruit flavors and a lemony backdrop that will flatter the spices in this menu.

1. Heat olive oil in a large skillet; sauté eggplant and onion until tender, about 5 minutes.
2. Add tomatoes, olives, wine, walnuts, raisins, tomato paste, vinegar, capers, salt, and pepper. Cook, uncovered, 15 to 20 minutes over medium-low heat, stirring occasionally. Stir in parsley. Serves 12.
—Chef Michelle Bernstein

PER SERVING: 130 CALORIES, 7G FAT, 0MG CHOL., 2G PROT., 13G CARBS., 4G FIBER, 240MG SODIUM

Mushroom, Artichoke, and Onion Matzo Kugel

If you don't have farfel on hand, simply break matzos into ½-inch pieces. While brands vary, a typical matzo makes about 1 cup of farfel. The kugel can be made a day in advance and baked for only 30 minutes. Allow it to come to room temperature and then bake 15 to 20 minutes, until thoroughly heated.

Cooking spray
10 large eggs
2 (15-ounce) cans lower-sodium chicken or vegetable broth, divided
1 (16-ounce) box matzo farfel (about 6 cups)
2 tablespoons olive oil
2 cups thinly sliced onion
1 tablespoon fresh rosemary
½ teaspoon dried thyme
½ teaspoon salt
4 cups sliced shiitake mushrooms
4 (6-ounce) jars marinated artichoke hearts, drained

1. Preheat oven to 350F. Coat a 13 x 9-inch baking dish with cooking spray.
2. Beat eggs lightly with 1 ½ cans broth. Stir in farfel and let stand.
3. Heat oil in a large skillet over medium-high heat. Add onions, rosemary, thyme, and salt; cook, stirring frequently, until onions are tender and lightly golden, about 6 minutes. Add mushrooms and cook, stirring, until tender, about 5 minutes. Remove from heat and stir in artichokes.
4. Stir vegetables into farfel mixture and transfer to the prepared baking dish. Bake 30 minutes; cover with foil and bake another 10 minutes. If kugel seems too dry, make several slits in the top with a butter knife and drizzle with extra broth. Serves 16.
—Marge Perry

PER SERVING: 340 CALORIES, 9G FAT, 135MG CHOL., 10G PROT., 57G CARBS., 4G FIBER, 380MG SODIUM

MUSHROOM, ARTICHOKE,
AND ONION MATZO KUGEL

APPLE FRITTERS

1	cup unsalted matzo meal
3	eggs
½	teaspoon salt
2	tablespoons vegetable oil plus more for frying
½	cup water
3	Granny Smith apples, peeled and diced
½	teaspoon ground cinnamon
	Pinch ground cloves
2	tablespoons sugar
	Honey and walnuts, optional

1. Beat matzo meal, eggs, salt, 2 tablespoons of oil, and water together in a medium bowl to form a batter. Stir in apples, cinnamon, cloves, and sugar.

2. Heat about 2 inches of oil in a heavy frying pan to 325F. Drop batter by the spoonful (*or use a small ice cream scoop*), about 5 at a time, into hot oil. Fry until golden brown on each side. Serve warm. Drizzle a little honey and sprinkle walnuts over fritters just before serving, if desired. Yield: 20 fritters.
—Chef Michelle Bernstein

PER SERVING (1 FRITTER): 150 CALORIES, 12G FAT, 30MG CHOL., 2G PROT., 9G CARBS., 0G FIBER, 70MG SODIUM.

NEW SPICE

Za'atar Bazaar
A pungent Middle Eastern spice blend, za'atar is made from sesame seeds, thyme, and sumac. It's the defining flavor in our Cornish hens. Look for it in ethnic markets labeled "Syrian marjoram" or "green thyme." It's great rubbed on roasted chicken or pork or whisked up with olive oil for a zesty dip with pita chips.

Easter Brunch

NO ONE KNOWS when the word "brunch," that delightful contraction of "breakfast" and "lunch," was officially coined. But the meal itself, a celebratory combination of both, began in 1884 New Orleans, when visitors to the Cotton Centennial Exposition discovered Begue's. Begue's served only one meal a day, at 11 A.M., when the city's hungry dock and French Market workers, at work since dawn, quit for the day. The Exposition tourists took to Begue's elaborate, multi-course breakfast for the same reasons we love brunch today: nothing says "laid-back" or "vacation" like a lazily late breakfast, with lush, out-of-the-ordinary food.

Eggs are the order of the day when it comes to brunch. Here they star in Herbed Spinach and Goat Cheese Strata. Whether you're celebrating Easter or spring's arrival, having friends in for the weekend, or all three, these easy dishes make any brunch festive and delicious.

—*Crescent Dragonwagon*

THE MENU

HERBED SPINACH AND GOAT CHEESE STRATA
STRAWBERRY PROSECCO COCKTAIL
SPRING FRUIT COMPOTE
RASPBERRY EASTER BREAD

HERBED SPINACH AND GOAT CHEESE STRATA
Prepare this strata the night before and pop it in the oven in the morning or let stand a couple of hours and then bake. It's also great for dinner with a big green salad.

1	(10-ounce) package frozen spinach, thawed
1	tablespoon olive oil
1	large onion, finely chopped
½	teaspoon salt, divided
	Coarsely ground black pepper
¼	teaspoon freshly grated nutmeg
8	cups cubed rustic bread, such as ciabatta (about a 1-pound loaf)
1 ½	cups (6 ounces) crumbled goat cheese
1	cup (4 ounces) shredded sharp Cheddar cheese
	Butter to coat baking pan
2 ¾	cups 2% reduced-fat milk
8	eggs
1 to 2	tablespoons whole grain mustard
2	teaspoons minced fresh rosemary
1	tablespoon minced fresh or ½ teaspoon dried thyme

WINE PICKS
Mouton Cadet Blanc is an inexpensive wine that stands up to goat cheese, as do many white Bordeaux. Or try a vernaccia such as Teruzzi & Puthod di San Gimignano Rondolino 2006. Like many lively Italian wines, it associates beautifully with bright, assertively flavored foods.

1. Place thawed spinach in colander to drain. Squeeze out excess water. Chop finely.
2. Heat oil in a large, heavy skillet over medium heat. Add onion and cook, stirring, until tender, 4 to 5 minutes. Add ¼ teaspoon salt, pepper, and nutmeg. Stir in spinach; remove from heat.
3. Toss bread cubes, spinach mixture, and cheeses together in a large bowl. Transfer mixture to a buttered 13 x 9-inch baking dish or 3-quart gratin dish.
4. Whisk together milk, eggs, mustard, and herbs. Add ¼ teaspoon salt and pepper. Pour evenly over bread mixture. Cover with plastic wrap and refrigerate overnight.
5. Preheat oven to 350F. Remove strata from refrigerator; let stand at room temperature 30 minutes.

6. Remove plastic wrap and bake, uncovered, about 45 minutes, until puffed, golden brown, and thoroughly cooked. Serves 10.
—Relish Chef Jon Ashton

PER SERVING: 310 CALORIES, 16G FAT, 200MG CHOL., 17G PROT., 22G CARBS., 1G FIBER, 670MG SODIUM

STRAWBERRY PROSECCO COCKTAIL

1 ¼	cups frozen sliced strawberries with sugar, thawed
1	(750ml) bottle Prosecco, chilled
6	small strawberries, for garnish

1. Purée sliced strawberries and any juice in a blender or food processor. Press mixture through a fine-mesh sieve into a bowl to remove any seeds; chill 30 minutes.
2. Combine strawberry purée and Prosecco in a large pitcher and gently stir to combine. Pour into 6 champagne flutes. With a sharp knife make a small slice in the bottom of each whole strawberry, about half the way through. Slide berry onto the rim of each glass. Serve immediately. Serves 6.
—Marge Perry and David Bonom

PER SERVING: 120 CALORIES, 0G FAT, 0MG CHOL, 0G PROT., 7G CARBS., 1G FIBER, 5MG SODIUM

SPRING FRUIT COMPOTE

½   cup Grand Marnier (or other orange liqueur) or orange juice
2   tablespoons orange marmalade
½   cup quartered dried apricots
    Grated rind and sectioned fruit of 1 navel orange
1   fresh pineapple, peeled, cored, and cubed
4   pints fresh strawberries, raspberries, blueberries, and/or blackberries

1. Combine Grand Marnier, marmalade, apricots, orange rind and sections, and pineapple up to 24 hours in advance.
2. Up to 1 hour before serving, rinse berries. Hull strawberries and slice. Leave blueberries and raspberries whole. Cut blackberries into halves if they are large. Toss berries, as gently as possible, with marinated fruit. Serves 10.
—Crescent Dragonwagon

PER (1-CUP) SERVING: 120 CALORIES, 1G FAT, 0MG CHOL., 2G PROT., 31G CARBS., 5G FIBER, 5MG SODIUM

RASPBERRY EASTER BREAD

A food processor makes quick work of the dough for this lush, buttery bread. You may use almond butter in place of the almond paste. Make the dough a day ahead and refrigerate.

Dough

1	cup 2% reduced-fat milk, scalded and cooled to lukewarm
⅓	cup plus 1 teaspoon sugar, divided
2	packages active dry yeast
½	teaspoon salt
3	cups all-purpose flour
½	cup (1 stick) butter, chilled and cut into small pieces
3	egg yolks
1	teaspoon vanilla extract
½	teaspoon almond extract

Filling

1	cup seedless raspberry jam or fruit-only spread
5	ounces canned almond paste, coarsely grated or finely chopped

Glaze/Finish

	Cooking spray
1	egg white
½ to ¾	cup sliced, chopped, or slivered almonds
2	tablespoons sugar, preferably coarse sugar such as turbinado

1. To prepare dough, combine warm milk, 1 teaspoon sugar, and yeast in a small bowl. Let stand until bubbly, about 10 minutes.

2. Combine remaining sugar, salt, flour, and butter in food processor. Pulse until well blended. Add egg yolks, yeast mixture, and extracts. Process 20 to 30 seconds until thoroughly mixed and dough forms a ball. Transfer to a medium bowl, cover tightly with plastic wrap, and refrigerate at least 4 hours or up to 2 days.

3. Remove dough from refrigerator about 1 ½ hours before serving. Coat a large baking sheet with cooking spray. Divide dough and form into two balls, using about two-thirds of dough for one and one-third for the other. Roll larger ball into a 12 x 9-inch oval about ¼-inch thick. Transfer to the baking sheet.

4. To prepare filling, spread jam on dough, leaving a ¾-inch margin; sprinkle almond paste over jam.

5. Roll out second portion of dough into a slightly smaller oval, and place on the first, covering the filling. Roll the edge of bottom dough up and over the edge of the top dough. Pinch seams to seal.

6. Slash a few decorative cuts in top. Cover with a clean cloth and let rise in a warm place until almost doubled in size, about 45 minutes. About 30 minutes into the rise, preheat oven to 350F.

7. Bake 15 minutes. Remove, brush top with beaten egg white, and sprinkle with almonds and sugar. Bake an additional 25 minutes or until golden and fragrant and shiny on top. Serve warm or hot. Serves 12.

—Crescent Dragonwagon

PER SERVING: 380 CALORIES, 16G FAT, 75MG CHOL., 8G PROT., 54G CARBS., 2G FIBER, 170MG SODIUM

CENTERPIECE IDEA

Think Spring!
Buy containers of wheat grass from your local supermarket and tie a colorful ribbon around the container. Place in a glass bowl. For an Easter theme, tuck colorful jellybeans or dyed eggs around the grass, and your centerpiece is done.

Cinco de Mayo Celebration

CINCO DE MAYO, the commemoration of General Ignacio Zaragoza Seguin's unlikely victory over the invading forces of Napoleon III in 1862, was at one time a purely local celebration in the south-central Mexican state of Puebla. It's such an important date there that the capital's formal name is Heroica Puebla de Zaragoza. The day has become the biggest celebration of Mexican pride in the southwestern United States and northern Mexico.

THE MENU

TORTILLA SOUP
SOUTH TEXAS VEGETABLE TACOS
WITH GOAT CHEESE
MOLE (FOR GRILLED CHICKEN BREASTS)
TRES LECHES CAKE

As with any holiday, food plays a big part, so it's fitting to open with a big communal pot of the Southwestern classic Tortilla Soup. And what's a celebration without cake? Although Tres Leches Cake (Three-Milks Cake) draws on influences from outside Mexico, such as Spain, Cuba, and Costa Rica, it became part of Tex-Mex tradition more than a generation ago—just in time to become a favorite of this revitalized holiday.
—*David Feder*

TORTILLA SOUP
There are as many tortilla soups as there are cooking styles in Mexico and the southwestern United States. This mild, tomato-based version combines a number of favorite Mexican flavors into an earthy soup worthy of a meal.

1	tablespoon olive oil
1	onion, chopped
3	garlic cloves, minced
1	teaspoon chili powder
2	teaspoons ground cumin
1	teaspoon paprika
1	teaspoon dried oregano
1	(28-ounce) can crushed tomatoes, undrained
4	cups lower-sodium chicken broth
2	cups water
8	(6-inch) day-old corn tortillas, cut into strips and baked until crisp
1	(15-ounce) can hominy, drained and rinsed
1	medium poblano, Anaheim, or jalapeño chile pepper, seeded and chopped
1	(15-ounce) can black beans, drained and rinsed
1 ½	cups shredded cooked chicken
¼	cup chopped fresh cilantro
1	teaspoon salt

Garnishes
Avocado slices
Shredded Manchego or Monterey Jack cheese
Sour cream

45

1. Heat oil in a large stockpot over medium heat. Add onion and garlic; sauté until tender. Stir in spices, tomatoes, broth, water, and half of tortilla strips. Bring to a boil, reduce heat, and simmer 10 to 15 minutes.
2. Stir in hominy, chile, black beans, chicken, cilantro, and salt. Simmer 10 minutes.
3. Pour soup into bowls and top with remaining tortilla strips, avocado, cheese, and a dollop of sour cream. Serves 8.
—Robin Noelle

PER (1 1/2-CUP) SERVING: 220 CALORIES, 4G FAT, 10MG CHOL., 10G PROT., 36G CARBS., 8G FIBER, 1110MG SODIUM

SOUTH TEXAS VEGETABLE TACOS WITH GOAT CHEESE
Serve with black beans and rice, if desired. If you have leftover vegetables, they're delicious scrambled with an egg or two (and served in a tortilla, of course) the following day.

2	large poblano chiles
2	tablespoons olive oil
1	large red onion, slivered
4	small zucchini, cut into half moons (about 3 cups)
½	teaspoon kosher salt
1	cup fresh corn kernels
2	teaspoons dried oregano
½	cup chopped fresh cilantro
2	tablespoons freshly squeezed lime juice
	Coarsely ground black pepper
8	corn tortillas
8	ounces goat cheese

1. Cut chiles in half, lengthwise. Place on a foil-lined baking sheet; broil 3 inches from heating element 8 minutes or until blackened and charred. Place in a heavy zip-top plastic bag; seal. Let stand 15 minutes. Peel and discard skins and seeds. Chop.

2. Heat oil in a large skillet over medium-high heat. Add onion, zucchini, and salt; sauté until lightly browned, about 7 minutes. Add corn; cook 2 minutes. Add oregano, cilantro, lime juice, and chopped chiles; cook, stirring, until thoroughly heated. Season with black pepper.

3. Heat tortillas one at a time in a dry cast-iron skillet over medium heat until softened and browned in spots. Spread each tortilla with 2 tablespoons of goat cheese, top with vegetable mixture, and serve immediately. Serves 4.

—Chef Paula Disbrowe,

PER SERVING: 480 CALORIES, 27G FAT, 45MG CHOL., 17G PROT., 45G CARBS., 6G FIBER, 610MG SODIUM

MOLE

Use this Mexican sauce on baked, grilled, or broiled chicken. Refrigerate any leftovers up to 1 week.

1 ½	ounces dried mulatto or pasilla chile, seeded
1	ounce dried guajillo chile, seeded
½	cup skinless peanuts
¼	cup whole almonds
1	cinnamon stick
¼	cup sesame seeds
1	(6-inch) corn tortilla, torn
3	tablespoons olive oil
1	large onion, diced
3	garlic cloves, minced
3	ounces Mexican chocolate (such as Ibarra or Abuelita), chopped
½	cup tomato sauce
2	teaspoons sea salt
¼	teaspoon coarsely ground black pepper
6	cups vegetable broth

1. Preheat oven to 350F.

2. Cut chiles into big chunks. Place chiles, peanuts, almonds, cinnamon, sesame seeds, and tortilla pieces on a baking sheet. Toast in oven 10 minutes.

3. Heat olive oil in a saucepan. Add onion and garlic; sauté 5 minutes. Add toasted nut mixture; sauté 5 minutes. Add chocolate, tomato sauce, salt, and pepper; sauté 3 minutes. Add broth; cook 20 minutes over low heat. Purée mixture in a blender in three batches 3 to 4 minutes per batch. Return mole to saucepan and simmer until thickened, about 15 minutes. Serves 8.

—Chef Jesus Gonzalez

PER (1/2-CUP) SERVING: 270 CALORIES, 17G FAT, 0MG CHOL., 7G PROT., 25G CARBS., 5G FIBER, 1,020MG SODIUM

WINE PICK

Though beer is the traditional accompaniment for spicy Mexican menus, a wine spritzer is a fresh approach. Pour a half glass (about 4 ounces) of a dry, crisp rosé into a wine glass or tumbler. Add a couple of ice cubes, fill with soda, and finish it with a lemon twist. Perfect with our Vegetable Tacos.

47

TRES LECHES CAKE

This porous cake soaks up the three "milks"—milk, condensed milk, and heavy cream—giving the cake a moist, custardy texture.

- ¾ cup (1 ½ sticks) butter, softened, plus more for coating the baking pan
- 1 ½ cups sugar, divided
- 1 ½ teaspoons vanilla extract, divided
- 5 eggs
- 1 ½ cups all-purpose flour, plus more for coating the baking pan
- 1 ½ teaspoons baking powder
- 1 teaspoon cream of tartar
- 1 cup whole milk
- 1 (12-ounce) can evaporated milk
- 1 (14-ounce) can sweetened condensed milk
- 2 cups cold heavy cream
- 1 tablespoon rum
  Fresh berries for garnish

1. Preheat oven to 350F. Lightly butter a 13 x 9-inch baking pan. Dust with flour, shaking out excess.

2. Combine butter and 1 cup of sugar in a large bowl. Beat with a mixer at medium speed until fluffy. Add 1 teaspoon vanilla. Beat in eggs one at a time, mixing well.

3. Combine flour, baking powder, and cream of tartar. Beat into butter mixture gradually. Spread batter in prepared pan. Bake 25 to 30 minutes, until a wooden pick inserted into cake comes out clean. Let cool.

4. Stir together milk, evaporated milk, and condensed milk. Pour 3 cups over cake. Reserve remaining milk mixture to serve with cake.

5. Combine heavy cream, remaining ½ cup sugar, remaining ½ teaspoon of vanilla, and rum. Beat until soft peaks form. Spread over cake. Refrigerate until ready to serve.

6. Pour reserved milk mixture onto dessert plates. Slice chilled cake into squares and transfer to dessert plates. Garnish with fresh berries, if using. Serves 16.

—Robin Noelle

PER SERVING: 440 CALORIES, 26G FAT,
150MG CHOL., 8G PROT., 45G CARBS.,
0G FIBER, 220MG SODIUM

Mother's Day Dinner

In 1914, when President Woodrow Wilson signed the order making Mother's Day an official holiday, people marked the occasion by attending church and writing loving letters to their moms. Before long, these activities gave way to cards, flowers, and presents. Even Anna Jarvis, the woman who had proposed Mother's Day, tried to curb the excesses. But it seems Americans wanted to give Mom a gift or take her to dinner.

THE MENU

ONION SOUP
ROASTED HALIBUT WITH BRUSCHETTA or
CHICKEN SALTIMBOCCA
CAESAR SALAD
POACHED PINEAPPLE SUNDAES WITH
CINNAMON WONTON CRISPS

In the spirit of Wilson and Jarvis's original idea, give Mom a day off from cooking duties. Our festive but restrained menu offers fresh flavor combinations in restaurant-quality dishes that are simple enough for the occasional cook.

ROASTED HALIBUT WITH BRUSCHETTA

Here is a main dish bruschetta (broo-SKEH-tah)—garlicky toast topped with flaky halibut steaks and tomato relish. The anchovies "melt" into the tomatoes creating a rich, flavorful topping.

- 6 tablespoons olive oil, divided
- 1 pound grape tomatoes, cut into halves
- ½ cup finely diced red onion
- 5 flat anchovies, canned in oil, drained
- 3 large garlic cloves, minced, divided
- ½ teaspoon salt, divided
  Coarsely ground black pepper
- 4 (6-ounce) halibut steaks
- 4 (¾-inch thick) slices crusty bread
- ½ cup thinly sliced fresh basil leaves (see chiffonade tip on page 5)

1. Preheat oven to 450F.
2. Heat 3 tablespoons of olive oil in a large skillet. Add tomatoes, onion, anchovies, and 2 minced garlic cloves; stir. Cook over high heat, stirring constantly, until thick, about 5 minutes. Add ¼ teaspoon salt and pepper. Keep warm.
3. Stir together remaining 3 tablespoons olive oil, garlic, and salt. Brush fish with half of oil mixture. Place on a rimmed baking sheet. Bake 10 minutes, or until fish turns opaque and flakes easily.
4. Brush both sides of bread slices with remaining oil mixture. Place on a rack set over a baking sheet and toast until golden brown, about 3 minutes.
5. Place a bread slice on each plate. Top with tomato mixture and fish. Sprinkle with basil. Serves 4.
—Rozanne Gold

PER SERVING: 440 CALORIES, 26G FAT, 50MG CHOL., 34G PROT., 17G CARBS., 2G FIBER, 670MG SODIUM

WINE PICKS
Raise a glass of pink sparkling wine to Mom. A blushing, sparkling pinot noir, such as a classic Blanc de Noirs, has the food-friendly effect of Pinot Noir and plenty of festive bubbles. If Mom likes her wine on the sweet side, reach for a Prosecco, the fruity and approachable sparkler from Italy.

Roasted Halibut with Bruschetta

ONION SOUP

A lighter version of French Onion Soup, this soup uses chicken broth in place of the traditional beef broth. If you plan to serve this with the Roasted Halibut with Bruschetta, you may want to omit the baguette slices and cheese.

2	tablespoons unsalted butter
3	cups thinly sliced Vidalia or sweet onions (2 large onions)
2	garlic cloves, minced
2½	tablespoons all-purpose flour
6	cups reduced-sodium chicken broth
1	cup white wine
¼	teaspoon fresh thyme
½	teaspoon salt
	Coarsely ground black pepper
6	baguette slices
½	cup shredded Swiss or gruyère cheese

1. Melt butter in a large saucepan or Dutch oven over medium heat. Add onions and garlic; cook until very soft and golden, about 20 minutes, stirring occasionally.
2. Sprinkle flour over onions, stirring to coat thoroughly. Add broth, wine and thyme; cover and simmer about 30 minutes. Add salt and pepper.
3. Top baguette slices with cheese and broil until melted. Ladle soup into bowls and top with baguette slices. Serves 6.

—Donna Shields

PER (1 1/4-CUP) SERVING: 210 CALORIES, 7G FAT, 25MG CHOL., 8G PROT., 23G CARBS., 2G FIBER, 960MG SODIUM.

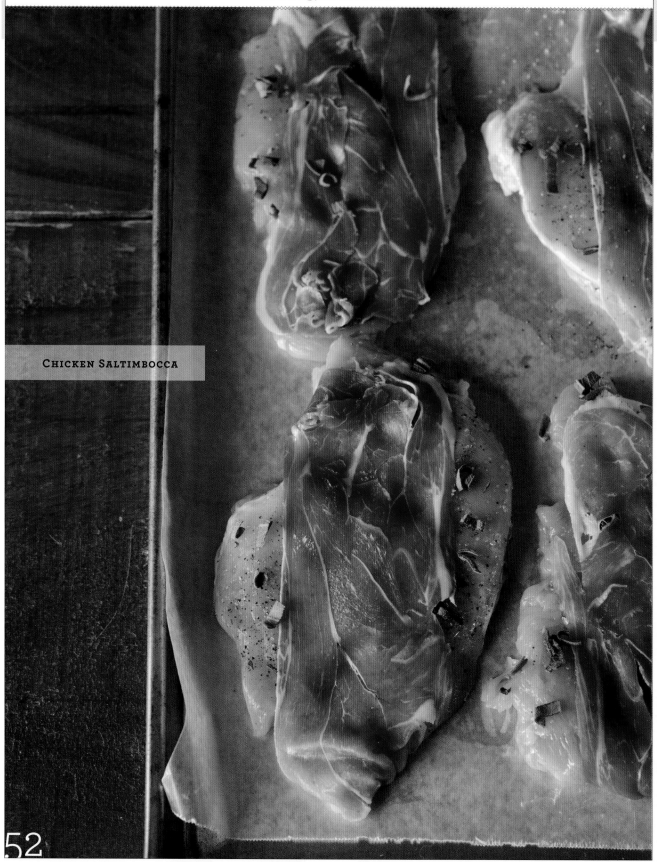

Chicken Saltimbocca

CHICKEN SALTIMBOCCA

4   (6-ounce) boneless, chicken breasts
½   teaspoon salt
    Coarsely ground black pepper
8   large fresh sage leaves, chopped
4   paper-thin slices prosciutto
½   cup grated Pecorino Romano cheese
⅔   cup all-purpose flour
2   eggs
¼   cup extra-virgin olive oil
    Fresh thyme sprigs
1   garlic clove, crushed
2   lemons, cut into halves

1. Preheat oven to 375F.
2. Pound chicken breasts to ¼-inch thickness with a meat mallet. Sprinkle each piece with salt and pepper. Top each with sage and cover with prosciutto. Press prosciutto so it will stick to the chicken.
3. Whisk cheese and flour together in a small mixing bowl and set aside. Beat eggs in a small shallow dish, such as a pie plate.
4. Heat olive oil in a large oven-proof or cast-iron skillet until hot. Add thyme and garlic.
5. Dredge chicken cutlets in cheese mixture to completely coat. Dip into beaten eggs. Dredge again in cheese mixture. Place in hot pan. Sauté until golden brown on both sides, about 2 minutes per side.
6. Place pan in oven and bake 10 to 15 minutes. Serve with lemon halves. Serves 4.
—*Relish* Chef Jon Ashton

PER SERVING: 440 CALORIES, 17G FAT, 225MG CHOL., 52G PROT., 16G CARBS., 0G FIBER, 1040MG SODIUM.

CAESAR SALAD

To streamline the dressing's preparation, we use pasteurized egg yolks here in place of coddling whole eggs. Make this salad just before serving and eat it with your hands as recommended by the salad's creator, Caesar Cardini.

7   tablespoons extra-virgin olive oil
4 to 6   garlic cloves, peeled and sliced thin
2 or 3   slices firm-texture bread, cut into bite-sized cubes (about 2 cups)
3   romaine hearts
½   teaspoon kosher salt
    Coarsely ground black pepper
    Juice from 1 lemon
2   pasteurized egg yolks
2   teaspoons Worcestershire sauce
½   cup freshly grated Parmigiano-Reggiano cheese

1. Combine olive oil and garlic in a small bowl; cover tightly and let stand 30 minutes to 1 hour.
2. Preheat oven to 325F.
3. Toss bread cubes with 3 tablespoons of garlic oil to coat. Spread in a single layer in a shallow baking pan. Bake

53

about 10 minutes, *(just until the edges begin to color. Set aside to cool.)*
4. Separate leaves of romaine hearts; place in a large salad bowl. Drizzle lettuce with 2 tablespoons more garlic oil, salt, and pepper; toss well. Add remaining 2 tablespoons garlic oil, lemon juice, yolks, and Worcestershire; toss gently. Sprinkle with cheese and croutons. Serves 6.

—Greg Patent

PER SERVING: 250 CALORIES 20G FAT, 75MG CHOL., 5G PROT., 12G CARBS., 1G FIBER, 390MG SODIUM

Poached Pineapple Sundaes with Cinnamon Wonton Crisps

Fresh pineapple slices are poached in a rose hip syrup and served over frozen yogurt with crunchy cinnamon-baked wonton wrappers. Wonton wrappers are available in the refrigerated or frozen food aisles of Asian food stores and in many supermarkets. If you prefer, coat them with cooking spray, rather than butter, to reduce fat and calories.

Wontons
- ½ cup sugar
- 1 ½ teaspoons ground cinnamon
- 32 wonton wrappers
- 4 tablespoons (½ stick) butter, melted

Sundaes
- 1 ripe fresh pineapple
- 5 cups water
- ½ cup honey
- 4 rose hip tea bags or 3 tablespoons dried rose hips
- 1 cup vanilla frozen yogurt

1. To prepare wontons, preheat oven to 400F.
2. Combine sugar and cinnamon in a small bowl.
3. Separate wonton wrappers and place on baking sheets, about ½ inch apart. Brush lightly with melted butter. Sprinkle evenly with cinnamon-sugar. Bake 5 to 7 minutes, until crisp and golden. Be careful not to overbake. Let cool on a wire rack. The wonton crisps will keep, covered, in an airtight container, for 3 days. Yield: 32 wontons.
4. To prepare sundaes, peel pineapple. Cut pineapple crosswise into 8 rounds. Cut out the core.
5. Place pineapple in a large skillet. Add water and honey. Bring to a boil. Add tea bags and lower heat to a simmer. Cover and cook just until pineapple is tender, about 20 minutes. Remove pineapple with a slotted spoon and place in a shallow casserole. Discard tea bags or strain liquid through a sieve.
6. Cook liquid over high heat until reduced to 2 cups. Pour syrup over pineapple. Cover and chill until very cold. Place frozen yogurt in serving dishes, top with pineapple, and drizzle with syrup. Serve with Cinnamon Wonton Crisps. Serves 4.

—Rozanne Gold

PER SERVING (WITH 2 WONTONS): 340 CALORIES, 5.5G FAT, 20MG CHOL., 4G PROT., 73G CARBS., 2G FIBER, 140MG SODIUM

55

Country Couture Cookout for Memorial Day

GRILLING SEASON BEGINS earlier and continues later in the year below the Mason-Dixon line. Folks get really creative with their outdoor cooking, tossing all manner of meats, fish, vegetables, even fruit, on the grill.

To honor the first days of summer, here is a menu that offers something different, yet still familiar. Corn gets dressed up with chipotle butter, biscuits with fresh rosemary, and catfish with pesto. If you're tired of burgers and dogs, strike up the grill for a menu that's just a little bit country.

THE MENU

PESTO CATFISH PACKETS
ROSEMARY BISCUITS
PROSCIUTTO-WRAPPED ASPARAGUS BUNDLES
GRILLED CORN WITH CHIPOTLE BUTTER AND CHEESE
CHEWY FLOURLESS CHOCOLATE COOKIES

PESTO CATFISH PACKETS
Catfish, pesto, and tomatoes are wrapped in individual aluminum foil packets and grilled.

¼	cup extra-virgin olive oil
8	(6-ounce) catfish fillets
½	cup prepared pesto
½	teaspoon salt
	Coarsely ground black pepper
1	pint cherry tomatoes, cut into halves
16	lime slices

1. Preheat grill.
2. Cut eight 12 x 8-inch sheets of aluminum foil. Drizzle 1 ½ teaspoons olive oil onto each piece of foil. Place fish on top of oiled foil. Lightly spread 1 tablespoon pesto over each fillet. Sprinkle with salt and pepper. Top with tomatoes and lime slices.
3. Seal the foil packets and set on the grill rack. Grill 10 minutes or until fillets are opaque and easily flake with a fork. Serves 8.
—Jill Melton

PER SERVING: 310 CALORIES, 18G FAT, 85MG CHOL., 33G PROT., 2G CARBS., 1G FIBER, 410MG SODIUM

SIMPLE SOLUTION

Iced Tea with a Punch
Spiked iced tea is a lighter alternative to heavy cocktails for summer entertaining and is not nearly as potent as so-called Long Island iced tea, which doesn't actually contain tea at all. Simply add 1 to 2 tablespoons bourbon, rum, or dry sherry to each serving of iced tea. **For a refreshing non-alcoholic option, like our Icy Fruit Tea, go to relishmag.com.**

57

CHEWY FLOURLESS CHOCOLATE COOKIES

1 ¾	cups powdered sugar, plus more if needed
½	cup Dutch-processed cocoa, plus more if needed
2	teaspoons cornstarch
¼	teaspoon salt
2	egg whites
1	cup coarsely chopped pecans or walnuts, toasted

1. Preheat oven to 300F.

2. Mix together sugar, cocoa, cornstarch, and salt in a large bowl. Gradually add egg whites, stirring with a spoon until mixture forms a dough. (*The mixture should be thick enough to form into balls; if not, add more powdered sugar and cocoa.*) Add nuts; mix well.

3. Form the dough into 15 balls. Place on a large, parchment-lined baking sheet. Bake 16 to 19 minutes, until glossy and crackled. Let cool completely. Yield: 15 cookies.

—Tamar Haspel

PER COOKIE: 110 CALORIES, 7G FAT, 0MG CHOL., 1G PROT., 16G CARBS., 1G FIBER, 45MG SODIUM

SLICE-AND-BAKE COOKIES

Having your own slice-and-bake cookies in the freezer ready to be baked at a moment's notice will make your friends think you're a whiz in the kitchen. Here's a quick and easy recipe for Lemon Slice-and-Bake Cookies.

Place 1 cup (*2 sticks*) butter in a mixing bowl. Using a mixer at medium speed, beat until smooth. Gradually beat in ½ cup granulated sugar. Add 2 cups cake flour (*½ cup at a time*) and mix well. Add 2 tablespoons finely grated lemon rind and mix well. Divide dough in half and roll into logs about 1 ½ inches in diameter. Roll each log in powdered sugar. Wrap in waxed paper and freeze. To bake, defrost dough slightly and slice into ¼-inch-thick rounds. Place on an ungreased cookie sheet. Bake 30 minutes at 300F, or until edges are golden. Yield: 3 dozen.

—Charmian Christie

SPRING / Country Couture Cookout for Memorial Day

In summer, the song sings itself.

SUMMER

63

Grilled Dinner for Father's Day

WHEN SUMMER ROLLS around, men who don't cook a meal from October to May break out the charcoal chimney. It must go back to Paleolithic gender roles: men hunt and women gather. These days, firing up the grill and grabbing the meat to throw on it are the closest most men come to spearing a mammoth.

Give Dad a break on Father's Day. Take away his tongs, bring him a nice cold drink, and take over the hunting as well as the gathering. Here's a grilled dinner that he might not make himself, but will love all the same. But remember, don't get hooked on playing with fire; he's going to want his job back next week.
—*Tamar Haspel*

THE MENU

GREEK FETA AND DILL SPREAD

FIRE-ROASTED CORN SALSA (WITH GRILLED STEAK) **or** CURRIED FISH AND WATERMELON KABOBS

RATATOUILLE AND CHEESE BAKE or GRILLED ASPARAGUS

AMARETTO PEACH COBBLER

CURRIED FISH AND WATERMELON KABOBS
While grilling the watermelon sounds odd, the heat concentrates its natural juices and lends a smoky taste to the sweet fruit.

	Cooking spray
1	pound watermelon
1 ½	pounds mahi-mahi, swordfish, tuna, or other firm fish
4	garlic cloves, minced
2	tablespoons olive oil
	Pinch ground turmeric
1	teaspoon ground cumin
1	teaspoon ground coriander
1	teaspoon hot chili powder
½	teaspoon salt
	Lime wedges

1. Preheat grill and coat the grill rack with cooking spray. Soak 5 wooden skewers in water 5 minutes.
2. Seed watermelon; cut into 2-inch chunks. Cut fish into 2-inch cubes. Thread fish and watermelon alternately onto the skewers.
3. Combine garlic and oil in a small bowl; brush on fish and watermelon. Combine spices; sprinkle on fish and watermelon, turning the skewers to cover evenly.
4. Place the skewers on the grill rack. Grill about 2 minutes on each side. Serve with lime wedges. Serves 5.
—Morgan Jarrett

PER SERVING: 180 CALORIES, 6G FAT, 85MG CHOL., 21G PROT., 8G CARBS., 0G FIBER, 330MG SODIUM

SIMPLE SOLUTION

Don't crowd the grill.
Leave enough room around each piece of food for air to circulate so that the food sears properly and so that your fire has the air it needs to fuel it.

65

GREEK FETA AND DILL SPREAD

Salty and pungent with feta cheese, this dip is best with sweet dippers such as red bell pepper strips and carrot sticks. Or use as a sandwich spread. We liked it rolled up with lavash (Armenian cracker bread), fresh spinach, red bell peppers, and turkey.

1 ½ cups (8 ounces) crumbled feta cheese
 ½ cup plain low-fat yogurt
 ¼ cup low-fat sour cream
 1 tablespoon freshly squeezed lemon juice
 3 garlic cloves, minced
 ¼ cup finely chopped fresh dill
 ½ teaspoon coarsely ground black pepper

1. Combine all ingredients in a blender or food processor; purée until smooth.
2. Transfer mixture to a bowl. Serve as a spread or a dip. Yield: 2 ½ cups.
—Relish Chef Jon Ashton

PER (1/4-CUP) SERVING: 80 CALORIES, 5G FAT, 25MG CHOL., 4G PROT., 3G CARBS., 0G FIBER, 270MG SODIUM.

GREEK FETA AND DILL SPREAD

FIRE-ROASTED CORN SALSA
Serve this salsa with grilled steak.

Cooking spray
2   large tomatoes
1   ear corn, husked
¼   cup finely chopped onion
1   jalapeño chile, diced
½   cup chopped fresh cilantro
1   garlic clove, minced
2   tablespoons freshly squeezed lime juice
¼   teaspoon cumin
½   teaspoon salt
     Coarsely ground black pepper

1. Preheat the grill and coat the grill rack with cooking spray.
2. Place tomatoes and corn on the grill rack over high heat, and grill, turning often, until lightly charred and tender, about 10 minutes. Remove from heat and let cool briefly.
3. Dice tomatoes. Cut kernels off corn. Combine tomatoes and corn kernels in a large bowl with remaining ingredients. Yield: 4 cups
—Peter Bronski

PER (1/2-CUP) SERVING: 30 CALORIES, 0G FAT, 0MG CHOL, 1G PROT., 6G CARBS., 1G FIBER, 150MG SODIUM.

RATATOUILLE AND CHEESE BAKE

	Cooking spray
2	medium eggplant
3	tablespoons olive oil, divided
1 ½	teaspoons kosher salt, divided
1	cup chopped onion
2	garlic cloves, chopped
2	red or yellow bell peppers, chopped
2	cups chopped cooked potatoes
1	(28-ounce) can diced tomatoes, drained
¼	cup chopped fresh basil
¼	cup chopped fresh parsley
2	tablespoons chopped fresh oregano
¼	teaspoon coarsely ground black pepper
15	ounces whole milk ricotta
½	cup grated Parmigiano-Reggiano cheese

1. Preheat grill and coat grill rack with cooking spray.
2. Cut eggplant into ½-inch slices on the diagonal. Toss with 1 tablespoon of olive oil and 1 teaspoon of salt. Place on grill rack and cook 5 to 7 minutes on each side. Let cool and chop.
3. Preheat oven to 350F. Heat 2 tablespoons of olive oil in a large skillet and add onion, garlic, and peppers; sauté 7 minutes.
4. Add potatoes, eggplant, tomatoes, basil, parsley, oregano, ½ teaspoon of salt, and pepper; stir gently. Combine ricotta and Parmigiano-Reggiano. Place half of vegetable mixture in a 2-quart baking dish, top with ricotta mixture, and add remaining vegetable mixture. Bake 30 to 40 minutes or until bubbling. Serves 6.
—Liz Shenk

PER SERVING: 290 CALORIES, 8G FAT, 40MG CHOL., 14G PROT., 23G CARBS., 4G FIBER, 670MG SODIUM

GRILLED ASPARAGUS

Cooking spray
1 pound fresh asparagus, trimmed
3 tablespoons olive oil
½ teaspoon kosher salt

1. Preheat grill and coat grill rack with cooking spray.
2. Place asparagus in a large, shallow dish. Drizzle on olive oil. Sprinkle with salt.
Toss asparagus to coat with oil.
3. Place asparagus on the grill rack or in a wire grill basket.
Grill 5 minutes, turning every minute, until brown in spots. Serves 4.

PER SERVING: 90 CALORIES, 7G FAT, 0MG CHOL., 2G PROT., 4G CARBS., 2G FIBER, 240MG SODIUM,

69

AMARETTO PEACH COBBLER

This is a double-crusted cobbler, better for scooping than slicing into wedges. To peel peaches, boil them for 1 to 2 minutes, drain, then chill in ice water. Remove from water and slip off skins with a paring knife.

Pastry

2	cups all-purpose flour
½	teaspoon salt
½	cup (1 stick) cold unsalted butter, cut into ¼-inch pieces
½	cup ice water, divided

Fruit

6	cups peeled and sliced ripe peaches (about 3 pounds)
½	cup sugar
1	tablespoon all-purpose flour
1 ½	teaspoons finely grated lemon rind
1	tablespoon freshly squeezed lemon juice
3	tablespoons amaretto
½	teaspoon ground nutmeg
¼	teaspoon salt
3	tablespoons unsalted butter, cut into small pieces
1	egg white, lightly beaten
	Cinnamon-sugar or turbinado sugar, optional

1. To prepare pastry, pulse flour and salt in a food processor fitted with a chilled steel blade until combined. Add butter and pulse until mixture resembles coarse meal. (*To mix the dough by hand, combine flour and salt in a medium bowl and cut in butter with a pastry blender or 2 knives until mixture resembles coarse meal.*) With processor running, add half of water, processing just until combined. Add enough remaining water to make a dough that holds together. Divide dough into halves and press each half gently into a 4-inch circle on plastic wrap. Wrap in plastic and chill 30 minutes.

2. Preheat oven to 375F.

3. To prepare fruit, combine peaches, sugar, and flour; toss well. Add lemon rind, lemon juice, amaretto, nutmeg, salt, and butter; toss well.

4. Slightly overlap 2 sheets of plastic wrap on a work surface. Place one chilled dough circle on the plastic wrap. Cover with 2 additional sheets of overlapping plastic wrap. Roll the dough to a thickness of ⅛ inch. Line a 2-quart casserole (*2 ½-inches deep*) with the dough, trimming to fit. Spoon fruit into the casserole.

5. Roll out remaining dough between the sheets of plastic wrap to a thickness of ⅛ inch. Place over fruit. Moisten the edges of the top and sides with a little water, press them together and flute decoratively. Cut several slits in top crust. Brush crust with egg white and sprinkle generously with cinnamon-sugar, if desired.

6. Place the casserole on a rimmed baking sheet and bake 45 to 50 minutes, until the top is golden brown and the filling is bubbling. Serves 8.

—Damon Lee Fowler

PER SERVING: 320 CALORIES, 15G FAT, 40MG CHOL., 5G PROT., 44G CARBS., 2G FIBER, 220MG SODIUM

WINE PICKS

Summer calls for something refreshing, but you'll want a wine with some structure to stand up to the grilled steak and bold spices. A well-chilled rosé in a crisp, food-friendly style will mesh well with all that's going on here. Try Marqués de Cáceres 2008 Rioja Rosado. With the Curried Fish and Watermelon, try Banfi Centine 2008 Rosé, a crisp, dry version of rosé with hints of luscious berry flavors. For a little tingly-zingly in a pink-hued spritz, pop open a bottle of Cristalino Brut Rosado Cava.

71

Farmstand Celebration

THE SOUTH IS famous for its "meat and three," a meal consisting of a meat and three sides. But truth is, lots of folks skip the meat and just get the three . . . or four or five sides. A quick look at the farmers' market in July shows why. Stalls are overflowing with ripe red tomatoes, juicy cantaloupe, fresh berries, okra, perfect peaches, field peas, and corn, all waiting for a quick sauté or turn at the grill. Southern cooks gussy them up with staples like country ham and pimiento cheese for a satisfying supper. It's Southern comfort at its best. Eat up, y'all.

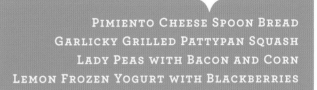

THE MENU

PIMIENTO CHEESE SPOON BREAD
GARLICKY GRILLED PATTYPAN SQUASH
LADY PEAS WITH BACON AND CORN
LEMON FROZEN YOGURT WITH BLACKBERRIES

PIMIENTO CHEESE SPOON BREAD

Use your favorite store-bought pimiento cheese in this savory spoon bread, a soft, soufflé-like side dish.

	Cooking spray
½	cup plus 2 teaspoons cornmeal, divided
1 ½	cups 2% reduced-fat milk
¼	teaspoon salt
⅛	teaspoon coarsely ground black pepper
3	eggs, separated
6	tablespoons pimiento cheese

1. Preheat oven to 375F. Coat a 6-cup soufflé dish with cooking spray; sprinkle with 2 teaspoons of cornmeal.
2. Combine remaining ½ cup cornmeal, milk, salt, and black pepper, to taste, in a medium saucepan; cook over medium heat until thick, about 5 minutes, stirring constantly. Remove from heat.
3. Gradually whisk egg yolks and pimiento cheese into cornmeal mixture. Pour into a large bowl; let cool completely.
4. Beat egg whites with a mixer on high speed until stiff peaks form. Gently fold into cornmeal mixture. Spoon batter into prepared dish. Bake 1 hour, or until puffy and browned. Serve immediately. Serves 4.
—Jill Melton

PER SERVING: 200 CALORIES, 10G FAT, 180MG CHOL., 10G PROT., 17G CARBS., 1G FIBER, 360MG SODIUM

GREAT TIP

$5 Gets You . . .
Here's a great tip from Jesse Cool, chef, cookbook author, and owner of Flea Street Café in Menlo Park, California. Give your kids $5 each and set them loose in a farmers' market. Tell them they can buy anything except bread and cookies. You'll be amazed at just how far $5 can go and at what they'll buy.

WINE PICKS
Spain's Albariño wines have lemony brightness, depth, fruit, and minerality. A good pick is Montecillo's Verdemar. For a domestic selection, try Carpe Diem Firepeak Vineyard Chardonnay 2006, from California's Edna Valley, which combines dynamic fruit and finish with refined sensibility.

73

Heirloom Watermelon
The seedless watermelons at the local grocery store are convenient, but if you can venture to your local farmers' market, look for more flavorful heirloom varieties. Keep an eye out for Moon and Stars and Carolina Cross. For a golden-fleshed watermelon, try Yellow Crimson.

Summer Picnic

THE MOVIE *PICNIC* wasn't about a picnic. Instead, it was about a slow dance on a dock, where Kim Novak's character realizes she's about to throw her rich boyfriend to the wind and follow a penniless drifter (William Holden) across America. Still, they had a picnic: cakes under domes, cold fried chicken, and coleslaw.

THE MENU

MEDITERRANEAN WATERMELON SALAD
SESAME NOODLES WITH SHREDDED VEGETABLES
LEMON-MARINATED CHICKEN BREASTS
ROASTED WALNUT AND SUN-DRIED TOMATO DIP
CHOCOLATE RANCH COOKIES

That was 1955. We still love a good picnic but need one that fits today's tastes and schedules. Lemony marinated chicken and sesame noodles are both made ahead and served cold or room temperature; piquant sun-dried tomato dip works as a dip or a sandwich spread. Cookies can be made days ahead, even frozen. Pack them up with a watermelon salad and you're set. Who knows? Maybe you'll get a slow dance on the dock.

—Bruce Weinstein and Mark Scarbrough

MEDITERRANEAN WATERMELON SALAD

½   red onion, thinly sliced
2   tablespoons freshly squeezed lime juice
1   pound watermelon
1   tablespoon honey
¼   teaspoon salt
    Coarsely ground black pepper
¼   cup extra-virgin olive oil
5   ounces arugula
2   tablespoons chopped fresh dill
3   tablespoons chopped fresh mint
4   ounces crumbled feta cheese
½   cup chopped pitted kalamata olives

WINE PICKS
Beaujolais-Villages is an easygoing red with lots of fruit but light on the puckery tannin. It's good served slightly chilled. For a white, Luna Vineyards Pinot Grigio is fruity with a nice citrusy angle.

1. Cover onion with lime juice.
2. Trim rind from watermelon and slice into ⅛-inch-thick pieces. Remove seeds.
3. Remove onions from lime juice. Add honey, salt, and pepper to lime juice; stir until well blended. Add oil, whisking, in a steady stream.
4. Arrange arugula on a large platter. Place watermelon and onion slices in overlapping layers on top of arugula. Top with herbs, feta, and olives. Drizzle with half of lime juice mixture. Pass remaining lime juice mixture at the table. Serves 6.
—Morgan Jarrett

PER SERVING: 200 CALORIES, 16G FAT, 15MG CHOL., 4G PROT., 13G CARBS., 1G FIBER, 470MG SODIUM

Fresh Heirloom
Tomato, Garlic &
Basil Sauce '08

STUFFED BAKED TOMATOES

4	tomatoes
6	tablespoons ricotta cheese
¼	cup chopped fresh spinach
1	garlic clove, minced
¼	teaspoon dried thyme
2	tablespoons finely grated Parmigiano-Reggiano cheese

1. Preheat oven to 400F.

2. Cut tomatoes in half crosswise. Combine ricotta cheese, spinach, garlic, thyme, and Parmigiano-Reggiano cheese. Top each tomato half with 2 tablespoons ricotta mixture. Arrange on a parchment-lined baking sheet and bake 10 to 15 minutes. Serves 4.

—Jill Melton

PER SERVING: 80 CALORIES, 3.5G FAT, 15MG CHOL., 5G PROT., 6G CARBS., 1G FIBER, 80MG SODIUM

SIMPLE NO-COOK TOMATO SAUCE

As the tomatoes marinate, they become juicier and juicier. Toss with pasta, spoon over chicken or beef, or simply eat with a spoon.

6	large fresh tomatoes
2	garlic cloves, chopped
3	tablespoons extra-virgin olive oil
⅓	cup chopped fresh basil
¼	teaspoon kosher salt
	Coarsely ground black pepper

Chop tomatoes and place in a large bowl.
Add garlic, olive oil, basil, salt, and pepper to taste. Toss gently.
Cover with plastic wrap and let stand at room temperature 2 hours. Serves 6.
—Liz Shenk

PER SERVING: 100 CALORIES, 7G FAT, 0MG CHOL., 2G PROT., 8G CARBS., 2G FIBER, 90MG SODIUM

YELLOW TOMATO SOUP WITH AVOCADOS AND CILANTRO OIL

This fresh tomato soup capitalizes on the numerous varieties of sweet cherry tomatoes. We thought the combination of yellow and red tomatoes was pretty, but you can use any color you like. If you're not a cilantro fan, substitute fresh basil.

Cilantro Oil
- 1 cup fresh cilantro
- ¼ cup extra-virgin olive oil

Soup
- 1 onion, chopped
- 2 tablespoons olive oil
- 2 cups yellow cherry tomatoes (or any summer cherry tomatoes)
- ½ teaspoon salt, divided
  Coarsely ground black pepper
- ½ cup red cherry tomatoes, chopped
- ½ cup black cherry tomatoes, chopped
- 1 avocado, peeled, pitted, and sliced

1. To prepare cilantro oil, place cilantro in a food processor or blender; process, adding olive oil until mixture is smooth and pourable.

2. To prepare soup, sauté onion in oil in medium saucepan over medium heat until translucent, 4 to 5 minutes. Add yellow tomatoes and cook until most of the liquid evaporates, about 20 minutes. Place mixture in a food processor or blender and process until well blended, about 2 minutes. Add ¼ teaspoon salt and pepper.

3. Place red and black tomatoes in a bowl. Add remaining ¼ teaspoon salt and pepper. Add 1 tablespoon cilantro oil. Toss to coat.

4. Serve soup, chilled or hot, topped with tomato mixture, slices of avocado, and a drizzle of cilantro oil. Serves 3.

— Chef Jon Ashton

PER (1-CUP) SERVING: 230 CALORIES, 19G FAT, 0MG CHOL, 3G PROT., 14G CARBS., 7G FIBER, 420MG SODIUM

GRILLED SHRIMP SKEWERS
WITH MINI SPINACH SALAD

Sizzling Summer Cocktail Party for Labor Day

FOR A THEME PARTY that's definitely not overdone, celebrate with the flavors of America's "51st state," the commonwealth of Puerto Rico. Puerto Rico's drinks naturally star rum and tropical fruit. The island's African and Spanish influences combine with local ingredients for dishes that blend fresh and fried, spicy and cool, and starchy and sweet. Our menu offers three appetizers, three drinks, and a dessert inspired by Puerto Rican flavors.

THE MENU

SUMMER RUM SLUSHES
MELON RUM PUNCH
LIME REFRESHER
GRILLED SHRIMP SKEWERS WITH MINI SPINACH SALADS
OMELET NACHOS WITH BLACK BEAN AND CORN SALSA
MEATBALLS IN SOFRITO SAUCE
PLANTAIN AND PINEAPPLE SUNDAES

SUMMER RUM SLUSHES

In Puerto Rico, rum is often mixed with fruit to create tasty blender drinks. This one uses a flavored rum that's just right for patio season.

¾	cup peach-flavored rum
1	(4-ounce) can frozen limeade concentrate, undiluted
½	cup pineapple juice
4 to 5	medium strawberries, hulled
2	cups ice
	Strawberry slices, for garnish

Combine rum, limeade, pineapple juice, and strawberries in a blender. With the blender running, add ice cubes, several at a time, through the lid. Blend until slushy. Pour into glasses and garnish with fruit, if using. Serves 6.
—Lisa Holderness and Wini Moranville

PER SERVING: 140 CALORIES, 0G FAT, 0MG CHOL., 0G PROT., 19G CARBS., 0G FIBER, 1MG SODIUM

MELON RUM PUNCH

Flavored rums have hit the market in recent years, making island-style rum punches better than ever. This one contrasts fresh tropical-fruit flavors with zippy citrus and bitters for pure refreshment—with a kick, of course.

3	cups guava nectar
3	cups pineapple juice
1 ½	cups melon-flavored rum
¼	cup grenadine
¾	cup freshly squeezed lime juice
2	teaspoons Angostura bitters
	Orange or lime slices
	Watermelon chunks or balls
	Maraschino cherries

PLANTAIN AND PINEAPPLE SUNDAES

While it may seem odd, the savory flavorings here—cumin, jalapeño, and green onions—add just the right exotic touch to these sweet sundaes. Plantains look like very large bananas but are much more starchy and require cooking. Choose a well-spotted, but not black, plantain. If it's too green (unripe), it will not peel easily.

½	teaspoon ground cumin
¼	teaspoon ground cinnamon
¼	teaspoon salt
1	medium-ripe large plantain, peeled and cut diagonally into ¼-inch-thick slices
3	tablespoons butter
1	cup bite-sized fresh pineapple chunks
6	tablespoons brown sugar
6	tablespoons red wine vinegar
2	green onions, thinly sliced
1	small jalapeño chile, seeded and finely chopped
3	cups vanilla ice cream

1. Combine cumin, cinnamon, and salt. Sprinkle on one side of plantain slices. Heat butter in a large skillet over medium heat. Add plantains, spice-side down; cook until golden and slightly softened, 2 to 3 minutes. Flip and cook 2 to 3 minutes. Stir in pineapple, brown sugar, and vinegar. Cook until thoroughly heated, 1 to 2 minutes. Stir in green onions and jalapeño; remove from heat.
2. Divide ice cream among 6 serving dishes. Spoon fruit and sauce over ice cream. Serves 6.
—Lisa Holderness and Wini Moranville

PER SERVING: 280 CALORIES, 13G FAT, 45MG CHOL., 3G PROT., 40G CARBS., 2G FIBER, 190MG SODIUM

DRESS IT UP

Decorating Your Table

To transport your guests to the tropics, try these decorating tips:

Visit your local florist, World Market, or Pier One for large banana leaves that can serve as placemats.

Fill glasses with turbinado sugar for the look of sand. Top with paper umbrellas.

The ultimate in luxury, look for sprays of orchids at your grocery's floral department.

What could be simpler than stacking a few vivid green limes in a clear glass vase.

.99

Youth is like spring, an over-praised season more remarkable for biting winds than genial breezes. Autumn is the mellower season, and what we lose in flowers we more than gain in fruits.
—*Samuel Butler*

FALL

Menus

Tailgating Party

TAILGATES ON THE BACKS of station wagons and pickup trucks originally were thought of as just a functional piece of the vehicle. But when Americans discovered how handy they were as serving tables, tailgating was born. When game day arrives, most tailgating parties extend way beyond the tailgate to tables, chairs, and grills. The key to tailgating—now that the tailgate is nonessential—is the portability of the food. Our menu is all make-ahead friendly and safe for a few hours at room temperature.

—*Jean Kressy*

THE MENU

BARLEY SALAD WITH ASPARAGUS AND RADISHES
STUFFED EGGS WITH RED ONION AND ANCHOVY
ROAST BEEF WRAPS WITH SWISS CHEESE AND CUCUMBER
CORNMEAL CAKE WITH MACERATED BERRIES

BARLEY SALAD WITH ASPARAGUS AND RADISHES

1	cup quick-cooking barley
½	pound asparagus, trimmed
2	celery stalks, diced
6	radishes, thinly sliced
⅓	cup finely chopped fresh parsley
2	tablespoons chopped fresh mint
2	tablespoons extra-virgin olive oil
2	tablespoons freshly squeezed lemon juice
1	tablespoon white balsamic vinegar
¾	teaspoon kosher salt
¼	teaspoon coarsely ground black pepper

1. Cook barley according to package directions. Transfer to a large bowl.
2. Cut asparagus diagonally into bite-sized pieces. (*You should have about 1 ½ cups*). Steam asparagus on steamer rack over boiling water until bright green and just tender, 1 ½ to 2 minutes. Place under cold running water; drain and pat dry with paper towels.
3. Add asparagus, celery, radishes, parsley, and mint to barley. Whisk together oil, lemon juice, vinegar, salt, and pepper in a small bowl. Pour over salad and mix gently. Serves 6.
—Jean Kressy

PER SERVING: 170 CALORIES, 5G FAT, 0MG CHOL., 4G PROT., 25G CARBS., 7G FIBER, 270MG SODIUM

STUFFED EGGS WITH RED ONION AND ANCHOVY

6 hard-cooked eggs
¼ cup mayonnaise
1 ½ tablespoons minced red onion
½ teaspoon anchovy paste
⅛ teaspoon coarsely ground black pepper

Slice eggs lengthwise into halves and remove yolks. Combine yolks, mayonnaise, onion, anchovy paste, and pepper in a medium bowl. Mash with fork to combine. Use a small spatula to fill egg whites with yolk mixture, mounding the tops. Yield: 12 stuffed eggs.
—Jean Kressy

PER SERVING: 70 CALORIES, 6G FAT, 110MG CHOL., 3G PROT., 0G CARBS., 0G FIBER, 120MG SODIUM

ROAST BEEF WRAPS WITH SWISS CHEESE AND CUCUMBER

Lavash, the thin flat bread also known as Armenian cracker bread, makes great wraps for picnic sandwiches. Look for it in packages near the deli counter.

½ cup mayonnaise
1 tablespoon sun-dried tomato paste
2 teaspoons horseradish
4 lavash breads
2 cups baby spinach leaves
½ pound thinly sliced deli roast beef
½ pound thinly sliced Swiss cheese
½ large seedless cucumber, peeled and cut lengthwise in 8 slices

1. Stir together mayonnaise, tomato paste, and horseradish in a small bowl.
2. Spread one lavash with one-quarter mayonnaise mixture down the long side almost to the edges. Top with one-quarter spinach, roast beef, and cheese. Top with cucumber slices. Fold in ends of lavash and roll up burrito-style. Wrap in plastic wrap. Repeat with remaining ingredients. Refrigerate until serving time. Cut each sandwich into halves to serve. Serves 8.
—Jean Kressy

PER SERVING: 300 CALORIES, 22G FAT, 50MG CHOL., 16G PROT., 11G CARBS., 1G FIBER, 380MG SODIUM

Cornmeal Cake with Macerated Berries

Cake

	Cooking spray
1	cup all-purpose flour
1 ½	teaspoons baking powder
¼	teaspoon salt
½	cup (1 stick) butter, softened
1	cup sugar
2	teaspoons grated orange rind
1	teaspoon vanilla extract
2	eggs
⅓	cup yellow cornmeal
½	cup 2% reduced-fat milk

Berries

1	cup each strawberries, blueberries, and raspberries
¼	cup sugar, or to taste
½	cup freshly squeezed orange juice

1. To prepare cake, preheat oven to 350F. Coat a 9-inch round cake pan with cooking spray.

2. Combine flour, baking powder, and salt in a small bowl.

3. Combine butter, sugar, orange rind, and vanilla in a large bowl; beat with a mixer at medium speed until evenly blended. Add eggs one at a time, beating after each addition. Reduce speed to low and add flour mixture and cornmeal alternately with milk, beating just until evenly incorporated. Scrape into prepared pan, spreading evenly. Bake 30 minutes or until a toothpick inserted in the center comes out clean.
Let cool in the pan on a wire rack.

4. To prepare berries, crush berries in a large bowl with the back of a spoon or a potato masher. Add sugar and orange juice and mix gently. Serve with cake. Serves 8.

—Jean Kressy

PER SERVING: 300 CALORIES, 13G FAT, 85MG CHOL., 5G PROT., 46G CARBS., 1G FIBER, 280MG SODIUM

SIMPLE SOLUTION

Buckets and Pails
Use buckets and pails to ice down beer and wine. For a simple ice bucket, line a bucket or pail with a plastic bag to hold ice for beverages.

Italian Grilled Dinner for Columbus Day

OCTOBER 12, 1492, the day Columbus's boats scraped ashore on Hispaniola, is a big day in Italian American communities. It commemorates not just Columbus, but all the great Italian explorers of the Americas: Vespucci, Verrazzano, Giovanni Caboto (John Cabot), and Malaspina.

THE MENU

POMODORO SAUCE
SAVORY POLENTA AND SAUSAGE
GRILLED SUMMER VEGETABLES
GRILLED PIZZA WITH MOZZARELLA AND POMODORO

Columbus Day falls on a Monday—not traditionally a day for a party, but a good one nonetheless. You can usually bet people are not otherwise engaged and excited to be invited—a party on a Monday! And in many parts of the country, it's still grilling weather on Columbus Day.

Celebrate all things Italian with this menu.

POMODORO SAUCE
Make this velvety sauce a couple of hours ahead. Use half on the pizza and serve the rest with the Savory Polenta and Sausage.

10	plum tomatoes, seeded and finely chopped
¼	cup finely chopped fresh basil
3	garlic cloves, chopped
1 ½	teaspoons sea salt
2	teaspoons coarsely ground black pepper
3	tablespoons olive oil

1. Combine all ingredients in a saucepan. Let stand 10 minutes.
2. Place over low heat; simmer until tomatoes are tender and mixture is thick, 20 to 30 minutes. Yield: 3 cups.
—Kristine Gasbarre

PER (1/4-CUP) SERVING: 40 CALORIES, 3.5G FAT, 0MG CHOL., 0G PROT., 2G CARBS., 1G FIBER, 290MG SODIUM.

SAVORY POLENTA AND SAUSAGE

Polenta
6	cups water
2	cups stone-ground grits (polenta)
½	cup grated Parmigiano-Reggiano cheese
3	tablespoons butter
2	tablespoons extra-virgin olive oil

Sausage Topping
	Cooking spray
1	pound bulk Italian sausage
1	tablespoon chopped fresh rosemary
1 ½	cups Pomodoro Sauce (see recipe above)

1. To prepare the polenta, bring water to a boil in a large saucepan and slowly add cornmeal, whisking constantly. Stir frequently over medium heat until polenta is thick and creamy, 15 to 20 minutes. Stir in cheese and butter. Pour olive oil in the bottom of a 13 x 9-inch baking dish. Spread polenta in pan. Allow to cool completely; chill overnight in refrigerator. Cut into 12 triangles.

2. Preheat grill and coat grill rack with cooking spray.

3. To prepare the sausage topping, cook sausage and rosemary in a skillet over medium heat until browned; stir to crumble. Drain.

4. Place polenta triangles on grill rack. Brown on both sides. Place 2 polenta triangles on each serving plate. Top each serving with 2 tablespoons Pomodoro Sauce. Scatter sausage on top. Serves 6.

—Kristine Gasbarre

PER SERVING: 485 CALORIES, 28G FAT, 50MG CHOL., 15G PROT., 40G CARBS., 3G FIBER, 990MG SODIUM

GRILLED SUMMER VEGETABLES

2	large zucchini
1	large yellow squash
3	red, yellow, or orange bell peppers
2	tablespoons extra-virgin olive oil
½	teaspoon crushed red pepper
1	teaspoon dried Italian seasoning or 1 teaspoon each fresh thyme, rosemary, and oregano
1	teaspoon kosher salt
	Coarsely ground black pepper
	Cooking spray

1. Cut zucchini and squash into thick slices on the diagonal. Cut peppers into quarters or large strips. Place in a large bowl; add oil, crushed red pepper, Italian seasoning, salt, and pepper to taste, and toss gently.

2. Preheat grill and coat the cooking rack with cooking spray.

3. Place vegetables on cooking rack and cook until crisp-tender and browned, about 7 minutes on each side. Serves 6.

—Kristine Gasbarre

PER SERVING: 80 CALORIES, 5G FAT, 0MG CHOL., 2G PROT., 8G CARBS., 3G FIBER, 350MG SODIUM

WINE PICKS

A Washington State syrah such as Barnard Griffin Columbia Valley Syrah is deeply fruity and its full flavor is good for pouring before dinner and with our pizza.

The tomato sauce in the sausage and polenta calls for Tuttobene Toscana Rosso IGT 2006, a merlot and sangiovese blend that brings deep fruit with nimble food-friendly acidity, or Pio Cesare Dolcetto d'Alba 2006, whose dark fruit flavors, sufficient tannin, and full body stand up to the tomatoes.

FALL / Italian Grilled Dinner for Columbus Day

GRILLED PIZZA WITH MOZZARELLA AND POMODORO

	Cooking spray
1	(10-ounce) prepared thin pizza crust
1 to 1 ½	cups Pomodoro Sauce (see recipe on page 109)
½	pound fresh or smoked mozzarella, cut into ⅛-inch slices

1. Preheat grill and coat cooking rack with cooking spray.
2. Place pizza crust upside down on the cooking rack and cook directly over medium heat until lightly browned, 5 to 10 minutes. Using tongs, flip the pizza crust over. Spread Pomodoro Sauce on crust and top with mozzarella slices. Grill, covered, about 10 minutes, or until the underside of the crust browns and the cheese melts.
3. Use two large spatulas to remove pizza from grill. Serves 6.
Note: If using fresh mozzarella balls packed in water, allow slices to drain between two paper towels before placing on pizza.
—Kristine Gasbarre

PER SERVING: 240 CALORIES, 7G FAT, 7MG CHOL., 18G PROT., 27G CARBS., 3G FIBER, 820MG SODIUM

KITCHEN TIP

Polenta versus Cornmeal
For the best polenta, use stone-ground grits or products labeled "polenta." Cornmeal, which many people use, is more finely ground than polenta and makes a mushier, gluey polenta, whereas more coarsely ground corn grits make a hearty, firm polenta. We like the corn grits (also marked "polenta") made by Bob's Red Mill.

113

Broiled Feta with Roasted Peppers and Olive Salad

United Nations Celebration

A GATHERING FOR United Nations Day, a little-known celebration inaugurated in 1948, gives you a really great reason to branch out to new kinds of foods and menus. Pick a cuisine you've enjoyed in restaurants but never tried cooking. Our Greek and Thai menus offer intense flavors in simplified recipes. A Greek meal of egg-lemon soup, broiled feta, roasted peppers, olive salad, and pears paired with yogurt is light but satisfying and rich in flavor. For a heartier menu, try our Thai menu: Thai Beef Salad, a Thai-style chicken curry, and a peanut sauce for dipping vegetables or tossing with noodles. Celebrate how easily the world comes together over a meal.

THE MENU

GREEK DINNER
Avgolemono (Greek Egg-Lemon Soup)
Broiled Feta with Roasted Peppers and Olive Salad
Greek Yogurt with Fresh Pears and Toasted Walnuts
THAI DINNER
Thai Beef Salad or
Panang Chicken Curry with Basil
Thai Peanut Sauce with Vegetables or Noodles

Avgolemono (Greek Egg-Lemon Soup)
Serve with warm pitas and store-bought hummus.

- 6 cups lower-sodium chicken broth
- ½ cup long-grain white rice
- 3 egg yolks
- 3 tablespoons freshly squeezed lemon juice
  Chopped fresh parsley
  Coarsely ground black pepper

Bring broth to a simmer in a large saucepan and add rice. Cover and simmer just until rice is done, about 15 minutes. Whisk egg yolks with lemon juice. Whisk a ladle of hot soup into egg mixture, then return mixture to pot. Season with parsley and pepper. Serves 6.
—Jo Marshall

PER (1-CUP) SERVING: 90 CALORIES, 2.5G FAT, 110MG CHOL., 4G PROT., 14G CARBS., 0G FIBER, 600MG SODIUM

Broiled Feta with Roasted Peppers and Olive Salad
Serve this salad with grilled pita wedges.

- 1 yellow bell pepper, cut into halves lengthwise
- 1 red bell pepper, cut into halves lengthwise
- 1 Vidalia onion, cut into thick rounds
- 1 head garlic, separated into cloves, peeled
- 1 teaspoon olive oil
- 8 ounces feta cheese
- 12 caper berries or 1 tablespoon capers

115

12   kalamata olives, pitted
12   cracked green olives or best-quality green olives, pitted
8   anchovy fillets
¼   cup coarsely chopped fresh parsley
¼   cup coarsely chopped fresh dill
¼   cup coarsely chopped fresh mint
¼   cup coarsely chopped fresh chives
3   tablespoons freshly squeezed lemon juice

1. Preheat oven to 400F.
2. Place peppers, onion, and garlic on a baking sheet. Brush onions with olive oil. Roast until peppers are charred and onions are tender, about 45 minutes. Transfer to a bowl and cover with plastic wrap. Let cool 15 to 20 minutes. Peel and slice peppers.
3. Preheat broiler.
4. Crumble feta into an 11 x 7-inch baking dish. Broil about 2 minutes, or until bubbling.
5. Combine remaining ingredients in a large mixing bowl. Add peppers, onions, and garlic. Toss to combine.
6. Spoon broiled feta onto serving plates. Top with pepper mixture. Serves 6.
—Chef Michael Psilakis

PER SERVING: 190 CALORIES, 13G FAT, 40MG CHOL., 8G PROT., 10G CARBS., 2G FIBER, 1,020MG SODIUM

GREEK YOGURT WITH FRESH PEARS AND TOASTED WALNUTS
Serve for breakfast or dessert.

1   cup water
1   cup sugar
1   cinnamon stick
1   star anise
4   peppercorns
2   pears, peeled, cored, and diced
2   cups Greek yogurt
½   cup walnuts, toasted and coarsely chopped

1. Combine water, sugar, spices, and pears in a medium saucepan. Bring to a boil. Reduce heat, cover, and simmer until pears are tender, about 10 minutes.
2. Place 1/2 cup of yogurt in each of 4 serving bowls. Top with pears and a little cooking liquid. Top with walnuts. Serves 4.
—Chef Michael Psilakis

PER SERVING: 300 CALORIES, 12G FAT, 10MG CHOL., 12G PROT., 42G CARBS., 5G FIBER, 40MG SODIUM

SIMPLE SOLUTION

Greek-Style Yogurt
Thicker, creamier, and higher in protein than typical American or European-style yogurt, Greek-style yogurt is available in large supermarkets. If you can't find it, you can make a pretty close approximation of it with plain whole-milk yogurt. Line a sieve with a clean linen kitchen towel or four layers of cheesecloth. Pour in the yogurt and let it drain, in the refrigerator, for 8 hours. The volume will reduce to about half, and the resulting yogurt will be almost as thick as a spread.

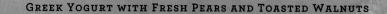

GREEK YOGURT WITH FRESH PEARS AND TOASTED WALNUTS

THAI BEEF SALAD

This main-course salad captures the essence of Thai cuisine. Full of contrasting textures (crisp greens, tender beef, crunchy peanuts) and tossed with a vibrant dressing, it's a bright, healthful dish that's alive with flavor.

¼	cup freshly squeezed lime juice
3	tablespoons fish sauce
1	tablespoon plus 1 teaspoon dark brown sugar
1	serrano chile or jalapeño chile, seeded and finely chopped
1 ¼	pounds flank steak
2	teaspoons peanut oil
¼	teaspoon kosher salt
	Coarsely ground black pepper
6	cups torn romaine lettuce
1	small red onion, halved and thinly sliced
½	English cucumber, halved lengthwise and sliced
¼	cup coarsely chopped fresh mint, divided
3	tablespoons coarsely chopped fresh cilantro, divided
⅓	cup coarsely chopped unsalted peanuts

1. Combine first four ingredients (*lime juice through serrano chile*) in a small bowl; whisk.
2. Preheat grill or broiler. Brush steak with peanut oil; sprinkle with salt and pepper. Grill or broil, turning once, until medium-rare, about 5 minutes per side. Remove from heat and let stand 10 minutes.
3. Combine lettuce, onion, cucumber, and half of both the mint and cilantro in a large bowl. Add all but

PANANG CHICKEN CURRY WITH BASIL

2 tablespoons of lime juice mixture. Toss well and mound on a large serving platter.
4. Thinly slice steak across grain and toss with remaining lime juice mixture. Arrange steak on top of salad. Sprinkle with remaining mint, cilantro, and chopped peanuts. Serves 4.
—Laraine Perri

PER SERVING: 360 CALORIES, 18G FAT, 60MG CHOL., 37G PROT., 15G CARBS., 4G FIBER, 1,120MG SODIUM

PANANG CHICKEN CURRY WITH BASIL
We used Panang curry paste by Taste of Thai, which comes in foil bags in the international aisle of the supermarket. Red or green curry paste can be substituted. Serve over jasmine rice so you won't lose a drop of the sauce.

1	(14-ounce) can light coconut milk
2	tablespoons Panang curry paste (1.75-ounce package)
1	tablespoon plus 2 teaspoons fish sauce
1	tablespoon plus 2 teaspoons dark brown sugar
1	tablespoon creamy peanut butter
1	tablespoon freshly squeezed lime juice
2	red bell peppers, seeded and cut into ¼-inch wide strips
1	red onion, cut into ¼-inch wedges
1	rotisserie chicken, skin removed, meat shredded (about 3 cups)
¼	cup chopped fresh basil
4	cups cooked jasmine or basmati rice

119

1. Heat a large sauté pan over medium heat. Add coconut milk, curry paste, fish sauce, brown sugar, peanut butter, and lime juice; whisk well. Add peppers and onion; stir to coat. Bring to a simmer, reduce heat, and cook, uncovered, until vegetables are crisp-tender, about 8 minutes.
2. Add chicken, cover, and simmer until thoroughly heated, about 5 minutes. Stir in basil; simmer 2 minutes. Serve over rice. Serves 8.
—Laraine Perri

PER SERVING: 320 CALORIES, 16G FAT, 45MG CHOL., 19G PROT., 26G CARBS., 2G FIBER, 360MG SODIUM

THAI PEANUT SAUCE

Try this creamy peanut sauce with grilled chicken or pork (a terrific way to introduce kids to Thai food), as a dip for cucumber slices, or tossed with a tangle of noodles. For more heat, increase the amount of crushed red pepper.

4	teaspoons peanut oil
⅔	cup minced shallots
4	garlic cloves, minced
½	teaspoon crushed red pepper
6	tablespoons creamy peanut butter
2	tablespoons hoisin sauce
2	teaspoons dark brown sugar
¾	cup water
1	tablespoon freshly squeezed lime juice

1. Heat oil in a heavy saucepan. Add shallot, garlic, and pepper; cook over low heat until fragrant and just beginning to color, about 3 minutes.
2. Whisk in peanut butter, hoisin sauce, brown sugar, and water. Bring to a boil, reduce heat, and simmer 1 minute. Stir in lime juice.
3. Serve warm or at room temperature. Yield: 1 ½ cups
—Laraine Perri

PER (2-TABLESPOON) SERVING: 80 CALORIES, 6G FAT, 0MG CHOL., 2G PROT., 6G CARBS., 1G FIBER, 130MG SODIUM

KITCHEN TIP

The Thai Pantry
The key ingredients in Thai cooking can be found in most supermarkets. Keep these on hand to infuse foods with Thai flavor:
Brown sugar
Rice
Cilantro
Limes
Hot Thai peppers
Coconut milk
Fish sauce
Thai-style curry pastes

121

RED APPLE SALAD WITH ORANGES AND FETA

Simple Supper by the Fire

SIMPLICITY IS A COZY chair, a drowsy cat, good conversation, and a well-made supper in a warm house. Let others brave the cold to go out; there's more comfort in quiet conversation and healthful food. Crisp apples, fragrant oranges, and salty feta compose a tempting salad. Braised chicken and vegetables is a classic for winter, with cornbread for those important pan juices. Apples appear again for dessert, broiled with maple syrup and apple brandy, because who can resist a warm baked apple on a cold night?

THE MENU

RED APPLE SALAD WITH ORANGES AND FETA
BRAISED CHICKEN AND VEGETABLES
BUTTERMILK CORNBREAD
BROILED APPLES WITH MAPLE AND BRANDY

RED APPLE SALAD WITH ORANGES AND FETA
Section the fruit over a large bowl to catch the juices and save some for the dressing.

- 3 seedless oranges
- 6 cups baby arugula
- 1 red apple, cored and thinly sliced
- 3 tablespoons freshly squeezed orange juice
- 2 tablespoons extra-virgin olive oil
- 1 tablespoon freshly squeezed lemon juice
- ¼ teaspoon kosher salt
- ⅛ teaspoon coarsely ground black pepper
- ½ cup (2 ounces) crumbled feta or blue cheese

1. Grate rind from 1 orange into a small bowl and set aside.
2. Working over a bowl, use a knife to cut peel and pith from oranges and cut fruit away from the membranes. Reserve juice, squeezing more for the dressing if needed. Combine arugula, orange sections, and apple in a large bowl.
3. Whisk 3 tablespoons orange juice, olive oil, lemon juice, salt, and pepper with orange rind. Pour over salad and toss gently. Spoon onto serving plates and sprinkle with feta. Serves 8.
—Jean Kressy

PER SERVING: 110 CALORIES, 6G FAT, 10MG CHOL., 3G PROT., 13G CARBS., 3G FIBER, 180MG SODIUM

WINE PICKS
Try Chateau de Lascaux du Languedoc, a blend of syrah and grenache from Vacqieres, France, or Zaca Mesa 2006 Z Cuvee, a California blend of grenache, mourvèdre, and syrah, to balance the fruity salad and savory chicken.

BRAISED CHICKEN AND VEGETABLES
This recipe is based on a traditional French dish. It uses inexpensive, flavorful chicken thighs and other pantry staples. Use an inexpensive, good-quality wine in this dish. We like the chardonnay from Mirassou.

- 1 tablespoon olive oil
- 6 bone-in chicken thighs
- 1 potato, peeled and chopped
- 1 yellow onion, finely chopped
- 2 carrots, chopped
- 2 garlic cloves, minced

123

¾	cup white wine (such as Chardonnay)
1	cup lower-sodium chicken broth
3	thyme sprigs
3	tablespoons freshly squeezed lemon juice
½	teaspoon salt
	Coarsely ground black pepper
1	tomato, chopped
½	lemon, thinly sliced, for garnish

1. Heat oil in a large, heavy skillet over medium heat. Add chicken and brown on both sides, 10 to 15 minutes. Remove chicken to a plate. Add potato, onion, and carrots to the pan; cook 5 minutes.
2. Return chicken to the pan (*with any juices*). Add garlic, wine, broth, thyme, lemon juice, salt, and pepper. Cover and simmer 15 to 20 minutes, or until chicken is cooked through. Add tomato and serve, garnished with lemon slices, if desired. Serves 4.
—Relish Chef Jon Ashton

PER SERVING: 320 CALORIES, 12G FAT, 75MG CHOL., 24G PROT., 21G CARBS., 3G FIBER, 540MG SODIUM

BUTTERMILK CORNBREAD
Combining the best elements of Northern and Southern cornbreads, this is a superb, just-barely-sweet version. Be sure to use stone-ground cornmeal for its full flavor and distinctive, delicious grittiness. If it's not available locally, it's worth ordering by mail. Two good sources: www.wareaglemill.com and www.bobsredmill.com.

	Cooking spray
1	cup all-purpose flour
1	cup stone-ground yellow cornmeal
1	tablespoon baking powder
¼	teaspoon salt
¼	teaspoon baking soda
1 ¼	cups buttermilk
2	tablespoons sugar
1	egg
¼	cup corn or canola oil
2	tablespoons butter

1. Preheat oven to 375F. Coat a heavy, ovenproof skillet with cooking spray.
2. Sift together flour, cornmeal, baking powder, and salt into a medium bowl.
3. In a smaller bowl, stir baking soda into buttermilk. Whisk in sugar, egg, and oil.
4. Place the pan over medium heat, add butter, and heat until butter melts and starts to sizzle. Carefully tilt pan to coat sides and bottom.
5. Pour wet ingredients into dry ingredients; combine quickly, using as few strokes as possible. Scrape batter into the pan. Bake 20 minutes, or until golden brown. Let cool 5 minutes. Cut into 8 wedges and serve. Serves 8.
—Crescent Dragonwagon

PER SERVING: 230 CALORIES, 4G FAT, 35MG CHOL., 5G PROT., 28G CARBS., 3G FIBER, 360MG SODIUM

BRAISED CHICKEN AND VEGETABLES

125

126

BROILED APPLES WITH MAPLE AND BRANDY

This recipe from Flagg Hill Farm in Vershire, Vermont, features the farm's signature apple brandy,
Pomme de Vie, inspired by the French apple brandy Calvados.

	Butter for coating the baking sheet
2	tablespoons unsalted butter, softened
4 to 6	apples, such as Jonagold, Northern Spy, or Cortland
	Juice of 1 lemon
4	tablespoons sugar, divided
⅓	cup maple syrup
3	tablespoons Pomme de Vie, Calvados, or other apple brandy
3	cups vanilla frozen yogurt

1. Preheat broiler. Lightly butter a baking sheet or shallow baking pan.
2. Peel, core, and cut apples into ¼-inch-thick slices. Evenly sprinkle lemon juice and 2 tablespoons of sugar over apples.
3. Place apples in a single layer on pan and broil about 6 inches from the heating element about 7 to 10 minutes until apples are golden. Remove pan from oven and sprinkle with remaining 2 tablespoons sugar. Return to the oven and broil until the edges just begin to darken or char slightly.
4. Place maple syrup in a small saucepan. Bring to a boil over medium-high heat. Add Calvados and cook 3 minutes, stirring frequently. Divide frozen yogurt amount 6 serving dishes and top with apples and sauce. Serve immediately. Serves 6.
—Flag Hill Farm

PER SERVING: 300 CALORIES, 8G FAT, 25MG CHOL., 3G PROT. 50G CARBS., 3G FIBER, 50MG SODIUM

KITCHEN TIP

Sectioning Citrus
Skinless and easy to eat, citrus sections are the best choice for compotes and salads. To section an orange or grapefruit, use a sharp knife to cut away the peel, pith, and outside membrane all at once to expose the fruit. Hold the fruit over a bowl and cut the fruit away from the membranes on each side of it. Squeeze the membranes to get every last bit of juice.

127

Happy Hour

FRIENDS ARE STOPPING by your place. You could spend hours in the kitchen whipping up patés and hors d'oeuvres. Or you could open a can of nuts, a bag of chips, and some store-bought salsa. But somewhere in between, there are easy-to-prepare and tasty foods that will keep you sane and make your guests feel special. These recipes are doable in 15 minutes flat and perfect for munching with beer, wine, or your favorite cocktail. Now that's a happy hour.

THE MENU

MISSISSIPPI CAVIAR
ROSEMARY-PARMESAN TWISTS
CASHEW BUTTERCRUNCH POPCORN
SPANISH-STYLE POPCORN
THAI-STYLE POPCORN
GOAT CHEESE AND ROASTED GARLIC DIP
SAVORY BASIL SLICE-AND-BAKES

MISSISSIPPI CAVIAR
With its sprightly, fresh taste, this salsa is perfect with chips or as a side to chicken, beef, or eggs.

- 1 (15-ounce) can black-eyed peas, drained and rinsed
- 1 (15-ounce) can black beans, drained and rinsed
- 1 (15-ounce) can whole kernel corn, drained and rinsed
- 2 large tomatoes, seeded and diced
- 1 onion, diced
- 1 green bell pepper, diced
- 3 tablespoons minced garlic (about 8 cloves)
- ½ bunch cilantro, chopped (about ½ cup)
- 1 jalapeño chile, seeded and finely chopped
- Juice of 1 lime
- 1 teaspoon dried Italian seasoning
- 1 (.7-ounce) package dry Italian dressing mix (such as Good Seasons)
- ½ cup extra-virgin olive oil
- ½ cup vinegar

1. Combine first 11 ingredients (*peas through Italian seasoning*) in a large bowl. Stir well.
2. Combine dressing mix, oil, and vinegar. Pour over pea mixture and stir well. Chill at least 2 hours.
Serve with tortilla chips. Yield: 8 cups
—Patricia Griffith

PER (1/2-CUP) SERVING: 130 CALORIES, 7G FAT, 0MG CHOL., 4G PROT., 14G CARBS., 3G FIBER, 430MG SODIUM

ROSEMARY-PARMESAN TWISTS

130

ROSEMARY-PARMESAN TWISTS

Puff pastry is a magic ingredient for busy cooks: it's elegant, delicious, and deceptively easy to work with. Serve with Chianti, wheat beer, or Bloody Mary's.

- 1 sheet (from 17.25-ounce package) frozen puff pastry, thawed
- 1 egg
- 1 tablespoon water
- ¼ cup (1 ounce) grated Parmigiano-Reggiano cheese
- 1 ½ tablespoons chopped fresh rosemary or 1 ½ teaspoons dried rosemary
- ½ teaspoon coarsely ground black pepper

1. Preheat oven to 400F. Line two baking sheets with parchment paper.
2. Roll puff pastry into a 14 x 10-inch rectangle. Whisk egg and water together and brush on pastry. Sprinkle with cheese, rosemary, and pepper, pressing them lightly into pastry.
3. Cut pastry into 24 strips, each slightly more than ½-inch wide. Gently twist each strip and place on prepared baking sheets. Bake 10 to 12 minutes, until golden. Serve warm or at room temperature. Serves 12.
—Gretchen Roberts

PER (2-TWIST) SERVING: 30 CALORIES, 2G FAT, 20MG CHOL., 1G PROT., 1G CARBS., 0G FIBER, 50MG SODIUM

CASHEW BUTTERCRUNCH POPCORN

Consider making this for the kids' Halloween party: a big bowl of crunchy, buttery kettle corn. Better yet, save it for the adults' party later on.

- 2 tablespoons canola oil
- ½ cup popcorn kernels
- ½ cup (1 stick) butter, plus more for coating the baking sheets
- 1 ½ cups salted roasted cashews
- 1 cup packed light brown sugar
- ¼ cup light corn syrup
- ½ teaspoon salt
- ¼ teaspoon baking soda

1. Heat oil in a large, deep saucepan. Add popcorn kernels; stir to mix well.
2. Partially cover pan but leave a small gap for steam to escape. Cook, shaking pan occasionally, until kernels have stopped popping, 4 to 5 minutes.
3. Remove from heat.
4. Preheat oven to 250F. Lightly butter 2 large, rimmed baking sheets; spread popcorn and cashews on sheets. Keep warm in oven.
5. Mix butter, brown sugar, corn syrup, and salt in a small saucepan; cook, stirring frequently, until sugar dissolves. Clip a candy thermometer to the inside of the pan and continue cooking undisturbed until temperature reaches 248F (*firm-ball stage*).
6. Remove from heat and stir in baking soda. The mixture will roil vigorously; continue stirring until well blended.
7. Remove popcorn and cashews from oven and drizzle evenly with hot sugar mixture; toss well with flat metal spatula or spoon.
8. Bake 45 minutes, tossing every 10 minutes. Let cool on baking sheet and store in a covered container at room temperature up to 3 days. Yield: 3 ¾ quarts
—Bruce Weinstein and Mark Scarbrough

PER (1-CUP) SERVING: 230 CALORIES, 13G FAT, 15MG CHOL., 3G PROT., 28G CARBS., 2G FIBER, 190MG SODIUM

SPANISH-STYLE POPCORN

Look for Spanish smoked paprika (pimentón) next to the sweet Hungarian paprika in the spice aisle of the supermarket.

3	tablespoons vegetable oil
½	cup popcorn kernels
½	teaspoon cumin seeds
1 ¼	teaspoon Spanish smoked paprika
¼	cup minced parsley
1	teaspoon salt

1. Heat oil in a large, deep saucepan. Add popcorn kernels and cumin seeds; stir to mix well.
2. Partially cover pan but leave a small gap for steam to escape. Cook, shaking pan occasionally, until kernels have stopped popping, 4 to 5 minutes.
3. Remove from heat. Add smoked paprika and parsley; mix well. Sprinkle with salt and serve immediately. Yield: 3 quarts.
—Monica Bhide

PER (2-CUP) SERVING: 120 CALORIES, 8G FAT, 0MG CHOL., 2G PROT., 13G CARBS., 3G FIBER, 390MG SODIUM

THAI-STYLE POPCORN

3	tablespoons vegetable oil
½	cup popcorn kernels
	Soy sauce
¾	teaspoon crushed red pepper
½	cup roasted peanuts
1	serrano chile, diced, optional
1	teaspoon salt

1. Heat oil in a large, deep saucepan. Add popcorn kernels; stir to mix well.
2. Partially cover pan but leave a small gap for steam to escape. Cook, shaking pan occasionally, until kernels have stopped popping, 4 to 5 minutes.
3. Remove from heat. Add a few splashes of soy sauce, crushed red pepper, peanuts, and chile, if using; mix well. Sprinkle with salt and serve immediately. Yield: 3 quarts.
—Monica Bhide

PER (2-CUP) SERVING: 190 CALORIES, 14G FAT, 0MG CHOL., 5G PROT., 15G CARBS., 3G FIBER, 520MG SODIUM

SIMPLE SOLUTION

How Much Wine Will You Need?
• A standard 750-milliliter bottle yields four to five glasses. Planning for up to one bottle per guest for dinner parties with multiple courses isn't off the mark.
• For cocktail gatherings, figure two glasses of wine per person for the first hour and one per person each hour after that.
• The more types of wine you serve, the less of each variety you'll need.
• If you're serving two different wines with dinner, figure one bottle for every two guests. For three different wines, figure one bottle for every three guests, and so on.

THAI-STYLE POPCORN

SPANISH-STYLE POPCORN

133

GOAT CHEESE AND ROASTED GARLIC DIP

GOAT CHEESE AND ROASTED GARLIC DIP
Use Montrachet or another soft, creamy goat cheese. For best flavor, refrigerate overnight before serving. Serve with pita or potato chips.

2	heads garlic
7	ounces soft goat cheese
½	cup low-fat sour cream
6	tablespoons light mayonnaise
2	tablespoons 2% reduced-fat milk
¼	cup chopped chives
½	teaspoon salt
¼	teaspoon coarsely ground black pepper

1. Preheat oven to 375F.
2. Cut off the top quarter of each garlic head. Wrap in foil and roast about 1 hour or until soft. Unwrap and cool 15 minutes.
3. Squeeze garlic pulp into a large bowl; mash. Stir in goat cheese, sour cream, mayonnaise, milk, chives, salt, and pepper. Cover and refrigerate overnight or up to 1 week. Yield: 2 cups.
—Bruce Weinstein and Mark Scarbrough

PER (1/4-CUP) SERVING: 130 CALORIES, 10G FAT, 20MG CHOL., 6G PROT., 4G CARBS, 0G FIBER, 340MG SODIUM.

SAVORY BASIL SLICE-AND-BAKES

If you like pesto, you'll love these savory wafers that contain the same ingredients. Perfect for parties.

- 2 cups all-purpose flour
- ½ teaspoon coarsely ground black pepper
- ½ teaspoon cayenne pepper
- ½ teaspoon salt
- ½ cup grated Parmigiano-Reggiano cheese
- 1 cup (2 sticks) butter
- 1 (8-ounce) package cream cheese
- ¼ cup prepared pesto
- ¼ cup fresh basil leaves, finely chopped
- 1 cup chopped walnuts, chopped almonds or whole pine nuts
  Kosher salt

1. Sift together flour, peppers, and salt. Stir in cheese.
2. Combine butter and cream cheese; using a mixer, beat until well combined. Add pesto and mix well.
3. Add flour mixture, basil leaves, and nuts. Mix well.
4. Divide dough in half and roll into logs 1½ inches in diameter. Roll each log in kosher salt. Wrap in waxed paper and chill until firm. If baking later, freeze shaped dough and defrost slightly before baking.
5. Preheat oven to 350F.
6. Slice dough ¼-inch thick. Place on ungreased cookie sheets. Bake 18 to 20 minutes, until edges are golden. Transfer to a wire rack to cool. Store in an airtight container in the refrigerator up to a week, or freeze up to a month. Makes 6 dozen.

PER WAFER: 60 CALORIES, 5G FAT, 10MG CHOL., 1G PROT., 3G CARBS., 0G FIBER, 55MG SODIUM.

KITCHEN TIP

How to Roast Garlic
Cut off the top quarter of a garlic head. Wrap in foil and roast at 375F about 1 hour or until soft. Unwrap and let cool 15 minutes. Squeeze garlic pulp into a bowl and mash.

THE MENU

PEANUT BUTTER SNACK MIX
ARUGULA SALAD WITH LIME, HONEY, AND MUSTARD DRESSING
BAKED RIGATONI WITH SAUSAGE, BUTTERNUT SQUASH, AND KALE or
CHICKEN AND FIG TAGINE WITH CILANTRO SALSA
PUMPKIN CUPCAKES WITH MAPLE CREAM CHEESE FROSTING
HALLOWEEN CANDY COOKIES

Abracadabra! Halloween Party

HALLOWEEN ORIGINATED as a time to celebrate the end of harvest. But what started as bobbing for apples and fortune-telling has become mostly a bonanza for the candy business. More candy is sold at Halloween than Valentine's Day, Christmas, and Easter. At last count, candy corn alone amounted to more than 20 million pounds.

As the kids have probably driven you crazy assembling their outfits, we've taken care of dinner. Peanut Butter Snack Mix gives antsy children at least one nutritious food before the candy. Serve the tagine as part of a neighborhood gathering, or as fuel for a couple of hours of trick-or-treating. Or let the slow cooker do its job, then when you return after a busy night of trick-or-treating, take off the mask and sit down to a bowl of stew, a fresh salad, and one of our cupcake cuties.

PUMPKIN CUPCAKES WITH MAPLE CREAM CHEESE FROSTING

Cupcakes
2 ¼   cups all-purpose flour
1   tablespoon baking powder
½   teaspoon baking soda
½   teaspoon salt
1   teaspoon ground cinnamon
½   cup (1 stick) butter, softened
1 ⅓   cups packed brown sugar
2   eggs
1   cup canned pumpkin
¾   cup 2% reduced-fat milk
¾   cup chopped walnuts or pecans

Maple Cream Cheese Frosting
¼   cup (½ stick) butter, softened
8   ounces cream cheese, softened
3   cups powdered sugar
½   cup maple syrup
2   teaspoons vanilla extract

1. To prepare cupcakes, preheat oven to 375F. Place 24 paper muffin cup liners in the cups of two muffin tins.
2. Sift together flour and next 4 ingredients (*baking powder through cinnamon*) in a medium bowl. Place butter and brown sugar in a large bowl; beat with a mixer at medium speed until light and fluffy. Add eggs, 1 at a time, beating well after each addition. Add pumpkin, beating on low speed. Add flour mixture and milk alternately to sugar mixture, beginning and ending with flour, beating on low speed. Stir in nuts.
3. Spoon batter into lined muffin cups, filling each about two-thirds full. Bake 25 minutes or until a toothpick inserted in the center comes out clean. Let cool 10 minutes in the pans on wire racks; remove from the pans. Let cool completely on the wire rack.

137

4. To prepare frosting, place all ingredients in a large mixing bowl; beat with mixer on medium speed until well combined. Spread frosting onto top of cooled cupcakes. Yield: 24 cupcakes.
—Karry Hosford and Julie Hession

PER SERVING: 280 CALORIES, 12G FAT, 45MG CHOL., 3G PROT., 41G CARBS., 1G FIBER, 220MG SODIUM

BAKED RIGATONI WITH SAUSAGE, BUTTERNUT SQUASH, AND KALE

Everyone will love this casserole, adapted from Lauren Bank Deen's Kitchen Playdates *(Chronicle, 2007). It's full of sausage, pasta, cheese, and squash all rolled into one yummy dish, perfect for Halloween.*

1 ½	pounds butternut squash (2 medium), peeled and cut into 2-inch chunks
1	tablespoon olive oil, plus more for coating the baking dish
6 to 8	sprigs fresh thyme
½	teaspoon salt, divided
	Coarsely ground black pepper
1	pound Italian sweet sausage, removed from casings
1	teaspoon fennel seeds
1	bunch of kale, tough stems removed and roughly chopped
6	garlic cloves, chopped
8	ounces rigatoni
2	cups half-and-half
½	cup lower-sodium chicken broth
1 ½	cups finely grated Pecorino Romano cheese
½	cup breadcrumbs
	Additional cheese for serving, such as grated Pecorino Romano or mozzarella

1. Preheat oven to 400F. Bring a large pot of water to a boil. Lightly oil a 13 x 9-inch baking dish.
2. Toss together squash, olive oil, thyme, ¼ teaspoon salt, and pepper on a large baking sheet. Roast 20 to 25 minutes, until squash is tender, but not mushy. Discard thyme.
3. Place sausage and fennel seeds in a large Dutch oven; cook over medium-high heat, stirring frequently to break up sausage, until meat is no longer pink. Remove sausage and drain most of oil. Place the pan over medium heat. Add kale and garlic; sauté until kale is wilted, 3 to 5 minutes. Add ¼ teaspoon salt and pepper. Remove from heat and add sausage to pan.
4. Reduce oven temperature to 375F.
5. Cook pasta in boiling water 2 minutes less than directions instruct. Drain well. Toss with sausage mixture. Add squash, half-and-half, chicken broth, and half of cheese. Gently toss. Transfer to baking pan, top with breadcrumbs, and remaining cheese.
6. Bake 25 minutes, until thoroughly heated and crusty on top. Serve with additional cheese at the table. Serves 8.
—Lauren Bank Deen's *Kitchen Playdates* (Chronicle, 2007).

PER SERVING: 460 CALORIES, 24G FAT, 60MG CHOL., 19G PROT., 39G CARBS., 3G FIBER, 880MG SODIUM

BAKED RIGATONI WITH SAUSAGE,
BUTTERNUT SQUASH, AND KALE

HALLOWEEN CANDY COOKIES

Here's some recycling you'll like—post-Halloween cookies. Chop up the candies and tuck the pieces into cookie dough in lieu of chocolate chips. Almost any candy will work. Standard chocolate chip cookies become immensely more interesting and the kids will have fun guessing what bits of candy are hidden within.

3 ⅔	cups all-purpose flour
1 ½	teaspoons baking powder
1 ¼	teaspoons baking soda
¾	teaspoon kosher salt
1	cup (2 sticks) butter
1 ¼	cups packed brown sugar
1	cup granulated sugar
2	eggs
2	teaspoons vanilla extract
2 to 3	cups chopped candy bits (such as jelly beans, Butterfingers, Baby Ruths, Heath Bars, Reese's Peanut Butter Cups, Twizzlers, M&Ms, and Lifesavers)

1. Sift flour, baking powder, baking soda, and salt into a large bowl.
2. Combine butter and sugars together in a large bowl; beat with a mixer at medium speed until very light, about 5 minutes. Add eggs, one at a time, mixing well after each addition. Add vanilla. Reduce speed to low. Add flour mixture and mix just until combined, 5 to 10 seconds. Stir in candy bits.
3. Preheat oven to 350F.
4. Drop dough by tablespoons onto a baking sheet. Bake 15 to 20 minutes. Let cool on baking sheet 2 minutes. Transfer to a wire rack to cool completely. Yield: about 4 dozen.

—Jill Melton

PER COOKIE (USING JELLY BEANS): 100 CALORIES, 4G FAT, 20MG CHOL., 1G PROT., 17G CARBS., 0G FIBER, 120MG SODIUM

ARUGULA SALAD WITH LIME, HONEY, AND MUSTARD DRESSING

You'll use only about one-third of the dressing for the salad. Refrigerate remaining dressing up to 1 week.

Dressing
- ¼ cup rice vinegar or white wine vinegar
- 1 shallot, finely chopped
- 2 tablespoons minced fresh cilantro
- 1 ½ teaspoons Dijon mustard
- 1 ½ teaspoons honey
- 1 teaspoon grated lime rind
- 1 teaspoon freshly squeezed lime juice
- ½ teaspoon grated peeled fresh ginger
- ½ teaspoon salt
- ⅛ teaspoon coarsely ground black pepper
- ¼ cup extra-virgin olive oil

Salad
- 6 cups arugula
- ½ cup chopped fresh chervil or flat-leaf parsley
- ½ cup chopped celery
- ⅓ cup chopped toasted almonds

1. To prepare the dressing, combine all ingredients in a small bowl. Whisk well.

2. To prepare the salad, combine all ingredients in a large bowl. Add ¼ cup of dressing. Toss well to coat. Serves 4.

—Jeanette Hurt

PER SERVING: 110 CALORIES, 9G FAT, 0G CHOL., 3G PROT., 6G CARBS., 2G FIBER, 70MG SODIUM

KITCHEN TIP

The Art of Salad
- Use a good homemade salad dressing.
- Dress the salad in moderation—don't drown the greens.
- Skip the watery lettuces and select flavorful greens such as arugula or mâche, spring mix, frisée, spinach, radicchio, watercress, and endive.
- Consider contrasts in your salad—sweet dried cranberries or raisins with sharp feta cheese or rich walnuts with bright crisp radishes or carrots.
- Toss the salad extensively. This way all the ingredients get coated with the dressing. (There's a reason it's called a "tossed" salad.) The more you toss, the less dressing you can use, and the fewer calories it will ultimately have.

Menus

HOLIDAY

Christmas is doing a little
something extra for someone.
—*Charles Schulz*

Coffee-and-Cake Dessert Buffet

IF THE COMMITMENT and workload of a dinner or cocktail party are too much for you, try gathering a group for relaxed conversation over coffee and cake. Wind down after a dinner out with friends over homemade Carrot Cake or Molten Chocolate-Chile Cakes or set up a dessert buffet of several cakes alongside coffee, cream, milk, and your favorite liqueurs and cordials. Or better yet, host a dessert potluck, asking your guests to bring their favorite treats—it's an easy solution for the busy host and a perfect way to kick off, or end, the holiday season.

THE MENU

KORY'S CARROT CAKE
MOLTEN CHOCOLATE-CHILE CAKE
APPLE CAKE
TENNESSEE WHISKEY CAKE

KORY'S CARROT CAKE
We made this cake in three 8-inch cake pans, but you can use two 9-inch cake pans instead. If using 9-inch pans, increase the baking time to 75 minutes. The food processor makes quick work of chopping the carrots.

Cake
4	eggs
1 ⅓	cups vegetable oil
2 ¼	cups sugar
2 ¼	cups all-purpose flour
2	teaspoons baking soda
2	teaspoons baking powder
½	teaspoon salt
2	teaspoons ground cinnamon
½	teaspoon ground cloves
½	teaspoon ground nutmeg
20	ounces carrots, finely chopped (about 3 ¼ cups)
½	cup chopped walnuts
1	cup crushed pineapple, well-drained

Frosting
3	(8-ounce) blocks cream cheese, softened
2	cups white chocolate chips, melted
¾	cup (1 ½ sticks) unsalted butter, softened
2	teaspoons grated lemon rind
	Chopped walnuts, optional

1. To prepare cake, preheat oven to 350F. Line bottom of three 8-inch round cake pans with parchment paper. The pans, even the sides, do not need to be coated with cooking spray.
2. Combine eggs and oil in a large bowl. Beat 2 minutes with a mixer on medium speed. Add 1 cup sugar and mix 2 minutes. Add remaining sugar and mix 3 to 4 minutes.
3. Combine flour and next 6 ingredients (*flour through nutmeg*) in a medium bowl; add to egg mixture, beating on low speed until blended, about 1 minute. Add carrots, walnuts, and pineapple; mix well.
4. Divide batter evenly among prepared pans.
5. Bake cakes 60 minutes or until a toothpick inserted in the center comes out clean.
6. Let cool to room temperature on a wire rack. Run knife around edge of cakes and remove from pans. Wrap in plastic wrap and refrigerate until ready to frost, up to 1 day.

149

7. To prepare frosting, place cream cheese in a medium bowl; beat with a mixer on medium speed until smooth, about 2 minutes. Add melted chocolate a little at a time, and beat at medium speed until combined, about 30 seconds. Add butter a little at a time and beat until combined, about 1 minute. Scrape down the sides of the bowl; add lemon rind and beat until combined.

8. Remove cakes from plastic wrap. Place one cake on a serving platter. Frost the top of the layer. Place the second cake layer on top; frost the top of the layer. Place the third cake layer on top; frost the top layer and the sides of cake. Press chopped walnuts, if desired, onto the sides of cake. Serves 20.

—Kory Rollison

PER SERVING: 552 CALORIES, 41G FAT, 100MG CHOL., 7G PROT., 42G CARBS., 1.6G FIBER, 392MG SODIUM

Molten Chocolate-Chile Cake

The combination of chocolate and chile is not a recent flavor pairing: The Mayans enjoyed chocolate and chile together for centuries. Here we use the rich, spicy duo in a molten cake. The joy of this dessert is in its make-ahead nature, which takes the stress out of entertaining. The batter of the cakes is divided into individual rame-kins and frozen, so on the big night, when dinner is wrapping up and you're getting ready to put the coffee on, you can pop the ramekins out of the freezer and right into the oven. The cakes are served hot, so there is no fussy cooling time to worry about. Although chipotle pepper may sound odd, it produces a nice kick, especially when accompanied by cooling vanilla ice cream. Use as much or as little of the pepper as you like.

	Cooking spray
½	cup sugar, divided
5 ½	ounces good quality semisweet chocolate (such as Ghirardelli), chopped
1	ounce unsweetened chocolate, chopped
10	tablespoons unsalted butter, softened
1 ½	teaspoons vanilla extract
1	tablespoon finely chopped canned chipotle pepper in adobo sauce
3	eggs
¼	teaspoon salt
3	tablespoons stone-ground cornmeal
2	tablespoons all-purpose flour
2	tablespoons unsweetened cocoa

1. Coat six 8-ounce ramekins with cooking spray. Coat each with 1 teaspoon sugar.

2. Place chocolates in bowl set over simmering water. Stir until chocolates melt. Remove from heat. (*Or place chocolate in a microwave-safe bowl. Microwave on medium about 30 seconds. Stir and repeat until chocolate melts. Let cool briefly.*)

3. Beat butter and sugar together in a large bowl with a mixer on medium speed until fluffy. Beat in vanilla and chipotle; the mixture may separate slightly. Add eggs, one at a time, scraping bowl and beating 1 minute, until thoroughly combined. Add melted chocolates and beat 5 minutes more. (*Batter will be thick.*)

4. Combine salt, cornmeal, flour, and cocoa in a small bowl; sift over batter and mix well.

5. Divide batter among ramekins. (*It's not necessary to smooth the tops.*) Cover each ramekin tightly with plastic wrap and freeze at least 4 hours.

6. Preheat oven to 400F. Place ramekins on a baking sheet. Bake frozen cakes 10 minutes.

7. Let the cakes stand 5 minutes. Invert onto serving plates. Serve immediately with vanilla ice cream and fresh raspberries. Serves 6.

—Crescent Dragonwagon

PER SERVING: 430 CALORIES, 31G FAT, 155MG CHOL., 7G PROT., 36G CARBS., 1G FIBER, 150MG SODIUM

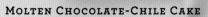
MOLTEN CHOCOLATE-CHILE CAKE

APPLE CAKE

	Cooking spray
8	tablespoons (1 stick) unsalted butter, divided
1 ½	cups sugar, divided
1	egg
1	cup all-purpose flour
1	teaspoon baking soda
½	teaspoon cinnamon
¼	teaspoon salt
2	large tart apples, cored and chopped
1	cup coarsely chopped walnuts
2	teaspoons cornstarch
¼	cup evaporated milk
1	teaspoon lemon juice
1	teaspoon vanilla extract

1. Preheat oven to 350F. Coat a 9-inch square baking pan with cooking spray.
2. Beat 5 tablespoons of butter and 1 cup of sugar with a mixer on medium speed until fluffy. Add egg and beat well. Stir in flour, baking soda, cinnamon, salt, apples, and walnuts. Batter will be stiff. Spoon into the prepared pan; smooth the top. Bake about 35 minutes, or until the center of the cake springs back when lightly pressed with a finger.
3. Combine remaining 3 tablespoons butter, remaining ½ cup sugar, cornstarch, and evaporated milk in a saucepan; bring to a boil over medium heat. Boil 2 minutes, stirring constantly. Remove from heat; stir in lemon juice and vanilla. Pour icing over hot cake. Serve warm. Serves 9.
—Candace Floyd

PER SERVING: 340 CALORIES, 20G FAT, 55MG CHOL., 5G PROT., 41G CARBS., 2G FIBER, 290MG SODIUM

KITCHEN TIP

Apples 101
- 1 pound of apples = 2 large, 3 medium, or 4 to 5 small apples
- 1 pound of apples = 3 cups peeled and sliced apples
- An average apple contains 80 calories, 18 grams of carbohydrates and 5 grams of fiber.

153

154

TENNESSEE WHISKEY CAKE

You can substitute 3 tablespoons water and 2 teaspoons vanilla extract for the whiskey.

- ½ cup (1 stick) butter, room temperature, plus more for coating the baking pan
- ½ cup packed brown sugar
- ½ cup granulated sugar
- 3 eggs
- 1 cup all-purpose flour, sifted
- ½ teaspoon baking powder
- ¼ teaspoon salt
- ½ teaspoon cinnamon
- ¼ teaspoon baking soda
- ¼ cup 2% reduced-fat milk
- ½ cup sorghum or molasses
- ¼ cup Tennessee whiskey, such as Jack Daniel's or George Dickel

1. Preheat the oven to 350F. Lightly butter a 9-inch springform pan. Wrap outside of pan securely with foil.
2. Combine butter and sugars in a large bowl. Beat with a mixer a medium speed until creamy. Add eggs, one at a time, beating well after each addition and scraping down the sides of the bowl.
3. Combine flour, baking powder, salt, cinnamon, and baking soda. Add to egg mixture alternately with milk, beginning and ending with dry ingredients. Stop mixer and add sorghum. Restart mixer and slowly add whiskey. Mix until smooth, about 30 seconds. (*Batter will be thin.*)
4. Pour into a baking pan. Bake 35 to 40 minutes, until a wooden pick inserted in the center comes out clean. Serve warm. Serves 8.

—Chef Jeff Carter

PER SERVING: 320 CALORIES, 14G FAT, 110MG CHOL., 6G PROT., 43G CARBS., 1G FIBER, 260MG SODIUM.

SIMPLE SOLUTION

High-Rise Dessert Service
Use wine or other stemmed glasses for desserts. Glasses do not need to match and are wonderful for dressing up desserts. They also offer just-the-right-size portions of spoonable, layered, or ice cream desserts.

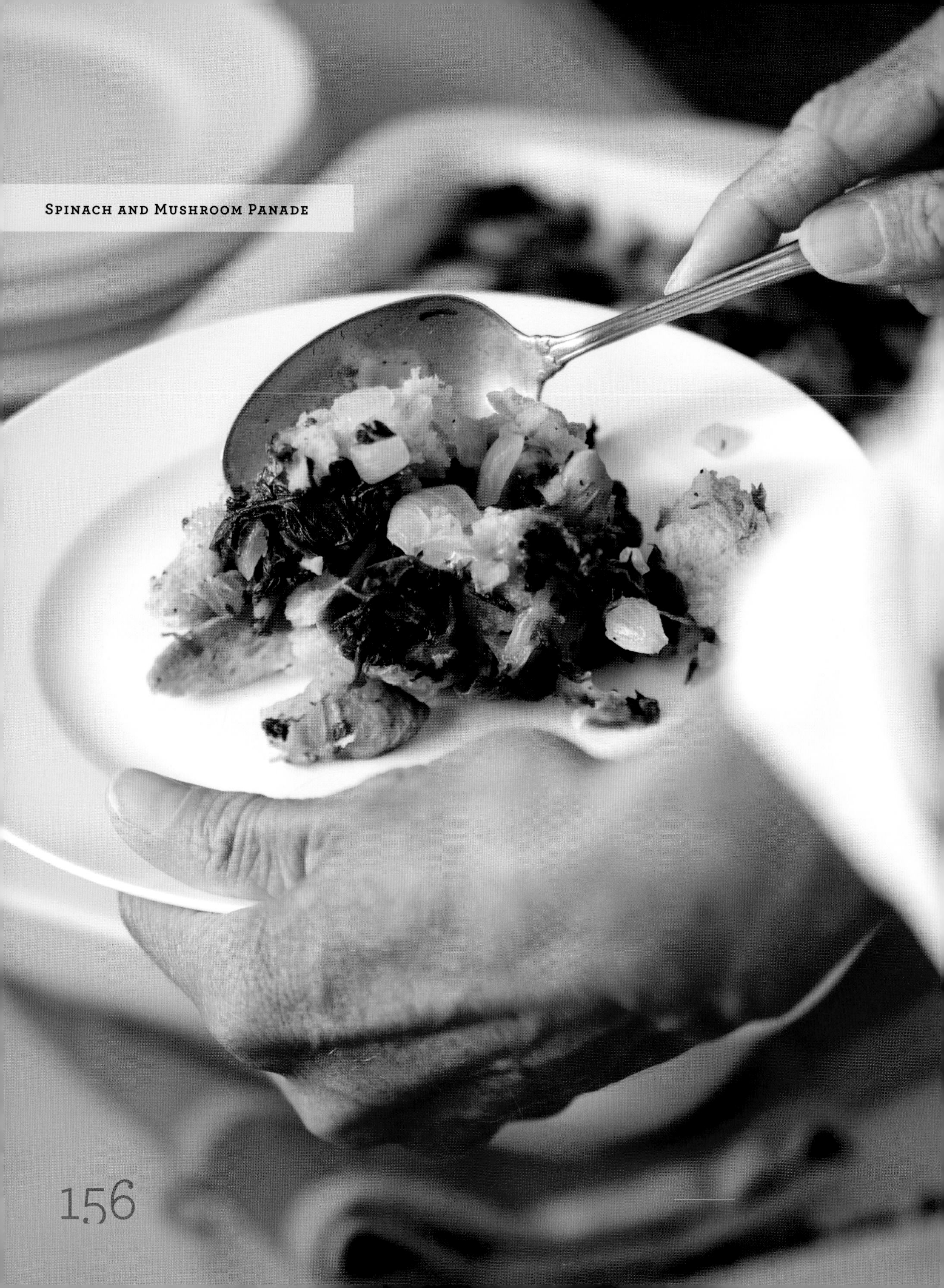

Spinach and Mushroom Panade

Thanksgiving: Three Menus to Be Thankful For

THANKSGIVING DINNER is easier on everyone if the menu matches the cook's skill and the guests' tastes. With that in mind, we offer three types of meals: an easy dinner for four, an epicurean dinner for twelve, and a vegetarian dinner for four.

THE MENU

EASY DINNER FOR 4
These easy-to-prepare versions of tried-and-true dishes include a few innovative twists.

PEAR SALAD WITH CRANBERRIES AND PECANS
SPINACH AND MUSHROOM PANADE
CITRUS-MARINATED ROASTED TURKEY
RUM-GLAZED CARROTS
BANANAS FLAMBÉ

EPICUREAN DINNER FOR 12
While this menu demands a little more shopping and cooking, you'll be rewarded with well-matched flavors in dishes that will surprise and delight.

MIXED GREENS WITH BLUE CHEESE AND CHAMPAGNE VINAIGRETTE
HERB-BRINED ROASTED TURKEY
OYSTER DRESSING
SAUTÉED MUSTARD GREENS
GARLICKY PUMPKIN AND BROCCOLI
POMEGRANATE-CHARDONNAY SORBET OR GRANITA **or**
BUTTERMILK PECAN PIE

VEGETARIAN DINNER FOR 4
This menu caters to an often overlooked guest at the Thanksgiving table: the vegetarian. No one will feel slighted with Vegetarian Harvest Tagine or the simpler Spinach Lasagna.

SPICED ORANGE SALAD
BUTTERNUT SQUASH SOUP WITH CARAMELIZED APPLE BRUSCHETTA
VEGETARIAN HARVEST TAGINE **or**
SPINACH LASAGNA
SPICED PUMPKIN PIE

157

Easy Dinner for 4

PEAR SALAD WITH CRANBERRIES AND PECANS

Sweet, juicy Bartlett pears are perfect for this salad. Ripen them on the counter until they have a delicious aroma, and then refrigerate them until it's time to make the salad.

3	tablespoons extra-virgin olive oil
2	tablespoons freshly squeezed lemon juice, divided
⅛	teaspoon salt
⅛	teaspoon coarsely ground black pepper
2	firm-ripe pears, such as Bartlett, cored and cut in bite-sized chunks
1	cup shredded or thinly sliced cabbage
¼	cup thinly sliced celery
¼	cup coarsely chopped pecans, toasted
¼	cup dried cranberries
6	cups mixed greens

1. Whisk oil and 1 ½ tablespoons lemon juice together in a small bowl. Add salt and pepper.
2. Combine pears and remaining lemon juice in a large bowl. Add cabbage, celery, pecans, cranberries, and oil–lemon juice mixture and toss gently to coat. Serve on mixed greens. Serves 4.
—Jean Kressy

PER SERVING: 200 CALORIES, 14G FAT, 0MG CHOL., 1G PROT., 20G CARBS., 4G FIBER, 80MG SODIUM

SPINACH AND MUSHROOM PANADE

The chewier the bread the better, so seek out a good artisan loaf. This recipe serves 12, but you'll want to have leftovers of this savory dish.

10	(½-inch-thick) slices country-style sourdough bread (about 12 ounces)
1	tablespoon extra-virgin olive oil
1	tablespoon butter
2	large onions, chopped
1	pound mushrooms, rinsed, stems trimmed, and sliced ¼-inch thick
2	garlic cloves, minced
¼	cup dry white wine
1	tablespoon minced fresh thyme or 1 teaspoon dried
1 ½	teaspoons salt
	Coarsely ground black pepper
1	(16-ounce) package frozen chopped spinach, thawed and well drained
	Cooking spray
1 ½	cups (6 ounces) grated Gruyère or Swiss cheese, divided
3 to 4	cups homemade or canned reduced-sodium chicken or vegetable broth

1. Preheat oven to 350F.
2. Tear bread into 1-inch pieces and toast on a large baking sheet until lightly browned, stirring once, 12 to 15 minutes.
3. Heat oil and butter over medium heat in a 12-inch skillet. When butter melts, add onions and cook 10 minutes. Increase heat to medium-high; add mushrooms, garlic, wine, thyme, salt, and pepper. Cook until liquid evaporates and mushrooms shrink, 10 to 15 minutes. Stir in spinach.

4. Preheat oven to 375F. Coat a 13 x 9-inch baking dish with cooking spray. Place half of bread in the prepared baking dish. Distribute half of vegetable mixture over bread and sprinkle on half of cheese. Repeat layers.

5. Slowly pour 2 cups of broth over the top, allowing bread to soak up broth and pressing with the back of a spoon. Add remaining broth until it reaches 1 inch below the pan edge.

6. Cover pan with aluminum foil and place on a baking sheet to catch drips. Bake, covered, 30 minutes. Remove foil and bake 35 to 45 minutes, until bubbling, puffed, and deep golden brown. Let stand 5 minutes before serving. Serves 12.

—Lynn Sampson Curry

PER SERVING: 190 CALORIES, 7G FAT, 20MG CHOL., 9G PROT., 19G CARBS., 1G FIBER, 720MG SODIUM

CITRUS-MARINATED ROASTED TURKEY

This turkey is steeped in a marinade of fresh orange juice, garlic, and rosemary, which is then used to baste the turkey. The marinade drips down into the pan making tasty drippings for the gravy. Serve with Citrus Gravy.

Marinade

½	cup grated orange rind (about 5 oranges)
4	cups freshly squeezed tangerine, clementine, or orange juice (about 8 oranges)
16	garlic cloves, crushed
1	tablespoon crushed red pepper
8	sprigs fresh rosemary
8	sprigs fresh thyme
2	tablespoons whole black peppercorns
½	cup extra-virgin olive oil

Turkey

1	(8- to 10-pound) turkey
1 ½	teaspoons kosher salt
	Coarsely ground black pepper

1. Combine all marinade ingredients in a disposable aluminum roasting pan large enough to hold the turkey and to allow marinade to rise high enough to coat about half of turkey. Rinse turkey well and pat dry. Sprinkle with salt and pepper. Place in marinade. Cover and refrigerate at least 2 hours, or overnight, turning turkey several times to evenly marinate.

2. Preheat oven to 450F.

3. Remove turkey from marinade. Strain marinade, reserving solids and liquid separately. Stuff solids into the cavity of turkey. Place turkey in the roasting pan. Pour liquid around turkey in pan. Roast 15 minutes. Reduce oven temperature to 350F and continue roasting, basting turkey every 30 minutes with pan juices, until an instant-read thermometer inserted into the thickest part of the breast registers 165F and the thickest part of the thigh registers 180F, about 15 to 20 minutes per pound. Let turkey stand 10 minutes before carving. Serves 8.

—Chef Ted Cizma

PER (6-OUNCE) SERVING, WHITE AND DARK MEAT: 290 CALORIES, 8G FAT, 130MG CHOL., 50G PROT., 0G CARBS., 0G FIBER, 120MG SODIUM.

Rum-Glazed Carrots

- ¼ cup (½ stick) butter
- 3 pounds whole slender carrots (about 16), trimmed
- ½ cup packed dark brown sugar
- ½ cup dark rum
- ¼ cup raisins
- ½ teaspoon coarsely ground black pepper

1. Melt butter in a large skillet over medium heat. Add carrots and toss to coat. Cook just until tender and beginning to brown, about 30 minutes, turning every 10 minutes.
2. Combine brown sugar, rum, raisins, and pepper in a small bowl; mix well. Pour over carrots. Reduce heat to low and cook 10 minutes, stirring occasionally. Spoon into a bowl and serve hot. Serves 8.
—Mary J. Lewis

PER SERVING: 190 CALORIES, 6G FAT, 15MG CHOL., 2G PROT., 26G CARBS., 4G FIBER, 120MG SODIUM

CITRUS GRAVY

2   cups reserved pan drippings from turkey
½   cup 2% reduced-fat milk
2   tablespoons all-purpose flour
¼   teaspoon salt
    Coarsely ground black pepper

Transfer turkey pan drippings from the roasting pan to a medium saucepan. Bring to a boil. Combine milk and flour in a small bowl, whisking until smooth. Whisk milk mixture into drippings, stirring until thickened. Add salt and pepper. Yield: 2 ½ cups gravy.
—Chef Ted Cizma

PER (1/4-CUP) SERVING: 190 CALORIES, 15G FAT, 5MG CHOL., 2G PROT., 12G CARBS., 0G FIBER, 290MG SODIUM

BANANAS FLAMBÉ

If using a gas stove, take pan off the heat before adding the rum.

2   tablespoons unsalted butter
¼   cup packed dark brown sugar
¼   teaspoon ground cinnamon
½   teaspoon freshly grated nutmeg
2   tablespoons banana liqueur
2   bananas, sliced in half lengthwise
¼   cup dark rum
    Juice of 1 lime

1. Melt butter in a large skillet over medium-low heat. Add brown sugar, cinnamon, and nutmeg; stir until sugar dissolves.
2. Add banana liqueur. Bring to a simmer and cook 3 minutes. Add sliced bananas; cook 1 minute on each side, carefully spooning sauce over bananas as they cook.
3. Carefully add rum and wave a long, lit match or stick lighter over the skillet until the rum ignites. Continue cooking, shaking pan slightly, until flame subsides, 1 to 2 minutes. Add lime juice and stir to combine. Serve over vanilla ice cream. Serves 2.
—*Relish* Chef Jon Ashton

PER SERVING (WITHOUT ICE CREAM): 410 CALORIES, 11G FAT, 30MG CHOL., 1G PROT., 57G CARBS., 3G FIBER, 5MG SODIUM

161

162

Epicurean Dinner for 12

MIXED GREENS WITH BLUE CHEESE AND CHAMPAGNE VINAIGRETTE

You'll use about half of the dressing and a quarter of the pecans. Store the remaining dressing in the refrigerator up to 1 week. Store the remaining pecans in an airtight container and serve as a quick appetizer.

Vinaigrette
- 2 tablespoons champagne vinegar or white wine vinegar
- 1 tablespoon Dijon mustard
- ½ cup bottled clam juice
- 1 garlic clove, crushed
- ⅓ cup canola oil
- ⅓ cup honey
- ½ teaspoon salt

Salad
- 18 cups mixed baby salad greens or spring mix
- 1 ½ cups dried cranberries
- 1 cup crumbled blue cheese
  Coarsely ground black pepper

Pecans
- 4 cups pecan halves
- 2 tablespoons olive oil
- 1 teaspoon kosher salt
- ½ teaspoon ground cayenne pepper
- 1 ½ teaspoons finely chopped fresh thyme
- 1 teaspoon finely chopped fresh rosemary
- ½ teaspoon coarsely ground black pepper
- ¼ cup packed dark brown sugar
- ¼ cup melted butter

1. To prepare vinaigrette, place vinegar, mustard, clam juice, and garlic in a blender and purée until smooth. Slowly add oil, blending until smooth. Add honey and salt; blend well.

2. To prepare pecans, preheat oven to 400F.

3. Combine all ingredients in a mixing bowl and toss until pecans are well-coated. Place pecans in a single layer on a baking sheet and bake 8 minutes. Yield: 4 cups.

4. To prepare salad, place greens in a large salad bowl. Add 1 cup of the pecans, cranberries, and blue cheese. Toss well. Drizzle with Champagne Vinaigrette and add pepper. Toss. Serves 12.

—Chef Doug Hosford

PER SERVING: 335 CALORIES, 26G FAT, 17MG CHOL., 6G PROT., 22G CARBS., 4G FIBER, 345MG SODIUM

WINE PICKS

Christian Moueix Merlot is a fruity, supple, and approachable wine from the owner of the renowned Chateau Petrus. For a white option, try a riesling from Germany. These wines stray toward sweet more often than New World rieslings, so look for the word "Kabinett" on the bottle to signal the off-dry variety. As an alternative to the merlot, try a grenache. A lively party pour, this good-time wine will fit right in with the merriment of the season. Look for Jaboulet "Parallèle 45" Rouge 2006 (Côtes du Rhône, France); Perrin Réserve Rouge 2007 (Côtes du Rhône, France); La Vieille Ferme Rouge 2007 (Côtes du Ventoux, France); Red Guitar Old Vine Tempranillo-Garnacha 2007 (Navarra, Spain); Rojo Garnacha 2007 (Valdepenas, Spain).

HERB-BRINED ROASTED TURKEY

Brining, or soaking the turkey in a salt-sugar-water solution, infuses moisture and flavor into the bird.
A large, clean cooler works well for brining. This recipe makes enough brine for a large turkey. For a smaller one
(8 to 12 pounds), make half the brine.

3	gallons hot water
3	pounds kosher salt
2	pounds sugar
¼	cup dried basil
¼	cup dried oregano
14	pounds ice
1	(15-pound) turkey, fresh or frozen, thawed
	Vegetable oil

1. Combine hot water and salt in a clean 12- to 15-gallon cooler. Stir until salt dissolves.
2. Add sugar, basil, and oregano; stir until sugar dissolves. Add ice and stir.
3. Place turkey in brine and cover with cooler lid. Soak overnight or up to 18 hours in a cool environment.
4. Preheat oven to 350F.
5. To prepare turkey, remove from brine and pat dry. Rub with vegetable oil. Place on a roasting rack and roast until the thickest part of the breast registers 165F on an instant-read thermometer and the thickest part of the thigh registers 180F. Remove turkey from the oven and let rest 15 minutes before carving. Serves 15.
—Chef Doug Hosford

PER (6-OUNCE) SERVING (WHITE AND DARK MEAT): 320 CALORIES, 12G FAT, 135MG CHOL., 49G PROT., 0G CARBS., 0G FIBER, 410MG SODIUM

OYSTER DRESSING

This Southern and Low Country specialty uses croutons instead of cornbread. Buy fresh oysters vacuum-packed in tubs with their juice, available at most seafood counters.

	Cooking spray
4	(5.5-ounce) boxes fat-free Classic Caesar–flavored croutons
1	cup chopped onion
2	garlic cloves, chopped
1	tablespoon chopped fresh dill
2	tablespoons butter, melted
¼	cup chopped flat-leaf parsley
2	eggs, lightly beaten
1	(10-ounce) package frozen spinach, thawed and drained
3	cups reduced-sodium chicken broth
1	(8-ounce) container freshly shucked oysters, chopped, and juice reserved
1 to 2	large bay leaves
1	teaspoon freshly squeezed lemon juice
	Coarsely ground black pepper

1. Preheat oven to 375F. Coat a 13 x 9-inch baking dish with cooking spray.

Herb-Brined Roasted Turkey

165

2. Combine croutons, onion, garlic, and dill in a large bowl; toss. Add butter, parsley, eggs, and spinach. Mix gently. Add broth, chopped oysters, and reserved juice. Add bay leaves, lemon juice, and pepper. Mix gently.
3. Transfer dressing to prepared baking dish. Bake 35 to 45 minutes. Remove bay leaves before serving. Serves 8.
—Claudia Carauna

PER SERVING: 400 CALORIES, 4G FAT, 60MG CHOL., 15G PROT., 60G CARBS., 1G FIBER, 1170MG SODIUM

Sautéed Mustard Greens
Hearty turnip greens or kale can be substituted for the mustard greens.

2	tablespoons vegetable oil
5	garlic cloves, minced
3	bunches mustard greens, washed, trimmed, and blanched
1	teaspoon salt
	Coarsely ground black pepper
6	slices thick-cut bacon, cooked and crumbled
1 ½	cup lower-sodium chicken broth

1. Heat oil over low heat in a large skillet. Add garlic and sauté 30 seconds. Add mustard greens, salt, and pepper. Sauté 3 minutes.
2. Add bacon and broth; simmer about 15 minutes. Serves 12.
—Chef Doug Hosford

PER SERVING: 100 CALORIES, 5G FAT, 5MG CHOL., 7G PROT., 10G CARBS., 6G FIBER, 440MG SODIUM

Garlicky Pumpkin and Broccoli
This Italian dish combines pumpkin chunks with broccoli in a garlic and red pepper–scented sauté. Butternut squash works just as well as pumpkin.

1	(2-pound) pumpkin
2	tablespoons olive oil
¼	teaspoon red pepper flakes
4	cups large broccoli florets
3	garlic cloves, chopped
½	teaspoon kosher salt
	Coarsely ground black pepper
½	cup grated Parmigiano-Reggiano cheese

1. Preheat oven to 350F.
2. Cut pumpkin in half, scoop out seeds and place, cut-side down, in a roasting pan. Add water to pan to a depth of 1 inch. Roast pumpkin about 45 minutes, or until tender. Scoop out pulp with a spoon and cut into chunks. You'll need about 3 cups of cooked pumpkin.
3. Heat oil and red pepper flakes in a large, heavy skillet over medium heat until oil starts to sputter and darken slightly.
4. Add broccoli, salt, and pepper and stir-fry 3 to 4 minutes. Increase heat to high; pour in ⅓ cup of water. Cover with a tight-fitting lid and steam 3 to 4 minutes.
5. Transfer to a baking dish. Scatter garlic and pumpkin over broccoli; stir well. Sprinkle with cheese and bake about 15 minutes, or until cheese melts. Serves 4 to 6.
—Crescent Dragonwagon

PER SERVING: 170 CALORIES, 11G FAT, 10MG CHOL., 9G PROT., 11G CARBS., 3G FIBER, 480MG SODIUM

GARLICKY PUMPKIN AND BROCCOLI

167

POMEGRANATE-CHARDONNAY SORBET OR GRANITA

4 ½   cups (36 ounces) pomegranate juice
1 ½   cups Chardonnay
⅔   cup sugar
    Pomegranate seeds for garnish

1. Place juice, Chardonnay, and sugar in a small saucepan over medium-high heat. Bring to a boil, reduce heat, and simmer 10 minutes. Remove from heat and chill thoroughly.
2. For a sorbet, pour into the canister of an ice-cream freezer; freeze according to manufacturer's instructions. For a granita, pour mixture into a 13 x 9-inch pan and freeze 8 hours, scraping occasionally with a fork. Spoon into a freezer-safe container; cover and freeze 1 hour or until firm.
3. Serve, garnished with pomegranate seeds, if desired. Serves 12.
—Chef Doug Hosford

PER SERVING: 110 CALORIES, 0G FAT, 0MG CHOL., 0G PROT., 23G CARBS., 0G FIBER, 15MG SODIUM

BUTTERMILK PECAN PIE

Pie Crust
1 ⅓   cups all-purpose flour
½   teaspoon salt
8   tablespoons vegetable shortening
3 to 3 ½   tablespoons ice water

Filling
3   eggs, room temperature
1 ⅓   cups sugar
2   tablespoons all-purpose flour
8   tablespoons (1 stick) unsalted butter, melted
¼   cup buttermilk
1   teaspoon vanilla extract
1   cup pecan pieces (or chopped pecans)

1. To prepare crust, combine flour and salt in a bowl; cut in shortening with a pastry blender or 2 knives until mixture resembles coarse meal. Sprinkle surface with ice water, 1 tablespoon at a time; toss with a fork until moist and crumbly. Press mixture gently into a 5-inch circle; wrap in plastic wrap. Chill 15 minutes. Flour dough lightly. Roll into circle between sheets of waxed paper on dampened countertop. Peel off top sheet. Flip into pie plate. Peel off other sheet and press pastry to fit into pie plate. Fold edge under and crimp or flute.
2. Preheat oven to 275F.
3. To prepare filling, beat eggs with a whisk. Add sugar and flour; beat well. Add melted butter, buttermilk, and vanilla. Stir well.
4. Sprinkle pecan pieces evenly into the pie crust; pour in egg mixture.
5. Bake about 1 hour or until golden brown and set. Serves 8.
—Pearson Farm

PER SERVING: 410 CALORIES, 29G FAT, 115MG CHOL., 5G PROT., 38G CARBS., 1G FIBER, 200MG SODIUM

BUTTERMILK PECAN PIE

169

Vegetarian Dinner for 4

BUTTERNUT SQUASH SOUP WITH CARAMELIZED APPLE BRUSCHETTA

While great paired with the soup, the bruschetta is also good served as an appetizer along with brie, Cheddar, or blue cheese and a crisp white wine.

Soup

- 2 pounds butternut squash, peeled, seeded, and cut into chunks (about 3 cups cubed)
- 4 cups lower-sodium vegetable broth
- 1 cup low-fat sour cream
- 1 tablespoon butter
- ¼ teaspoon ground cayenne
- ½ teaspoon kosher salt
  White pepper
- 1 tablespoon sugar (optional)
  Chopped fresh chives for garnish

Bruschetta

- 2 tablespoons butter
- 2 tablespoons extra-virgin olive oil, plus more for brushing toasts
- 3 apples, peeled, cored, and diced into quarter-inch cubes
- 2 tablespoons sugar
- 1 teaspoon cinnamon
- 1 baguette, sliced on the bias, into ¾-inch slices
- 1 garlic clove, halved
- ¼ teaspoon finely ground sea salt
  Coarsely ground black pepper
- 1 tablespoon honey

1. To prepare soup, combine squash and broth in a large saucepan; bring to a boil over high heat. Reduce heat to medium, cover, and simmer until squash is tender, about 20 minutes. Uncover and let cool.

2. Purée squash in a blender or food processor.

3. Return purée to saucepan and place over medium-low heat. Stir in sour cream, butter, and cayenne. Add salt and white pepper. If squash lacks sweetness, add sugar.

4. Cook soup just until heated through but not boiling.

5. To prepare bruschetta, warm a large sauté pan over low heat. Add butter and olive oil. Add apples; cook until tender, about 6 minutes. Add sugar and cinnamon; cook, stirring frequently, 8 minutes.

6. Preheat broiler.

7. Place bread on a large baking pan. Broil until golden brown, about 2 minutes per side. Rub each slice of toasted bread with cut-side of garlic and brush with a little olive oil. Sprinkle with salt and pepper.

8. Carefully drizzle a small amount of honey over toasted bread. Place a spoonful of apple mixture on top of each slice.

9. Ladle soup into bowls and garnish with chives and Caramelized Apple Bruschetta, if using. Serves 6.

—*Relish* Chef Jon Ashton

PER (1 1/2-CUP) SERVING (SOUP): 130 CALORIES, 8G FAT, 25MG CHOL., 5G PROT., 12G CARBS., 1G FIBER, 610MG SODIUM

PER (1-SLICE) BRUSCHETTA: 180 CALORIES, 5G FAT, 5MG CHOL., 5G PROT., 31G CARBS., 2G FIBER, 300MG SODIUM

VEGETARIAN HARVEST TAGINE

A tagine (TAH-jeen) is a conical dish used to make the Moroccan stew of the same name. Fortunately you don't need a tagine to make one, just a large pot, Dutch oven, or even a slow cooker. In fact, one of the best ways to make a tagine is in the slow cooker, which allows all the flavors to mix and mingle and . . . well, stew. While many tagines contain beef or lamb, this one is vegetarian, with garbanzo beans taking center stage. Serve over couscous.

2	tablespoons olive oil
1 ½	teaspoons butter
1	large onion, coarsely chopped
3	garlic cloves, minced
1 ½	teaspoons turmeric
2	teaspoons cumin seed
2	teaspoons coarsely ground black pepper
¼	teaspoon crushed red pepper
1	(14.5-ounce) can whole tomatoes, coarsely chopped, undrained
6	cups lower-sodium vegetable broth
½	teaspoon salt
1	(15-ounce) can garbanzo beans, drained and rinsed
2	large sweet potatoes, peeled and cut into 1-inch cubes
¾	cup golden raisins
½	pound green beans, cut into 2-inch pieces
1	zucchini, quartered lengthwise and cut into 2-inch pieces
1	unpeeled eggplant, coarsely chopped

1. Heat olive oil and butter in a large nonstick skillet. Add onion; sauté 3 minutes. Add garlic, turmeric, cumin, pepper, and crushed red pepper; sauté 3 minutes.

2. Transfer onion mixture to a slow cooker, along with tomatoes and their juice, vegetable broth, and salt. Cover and cook on high 1 hour.

3. Add garbanzo beans, sweet potatoes, raisins, green beans, zucchini, and eggplant. Continue cooking on high 1 ½ hours or on low 2 to 3 hours, until vegetables are tender. Serve over couscous. Serves 6.

—Crescent Dragonwagon

PER SERVING: 310 CALORIES, 8G FAT, 5MG CHOL., 9G PROT., 55G CARBS., 13G FIBER, 580MG SODIUM

SPICED ORANGE SALAD

Spicy dressing tops plump orange slices in this Moroccan salad. Serve chilled or at room temperature.

- 3   large navel oranges
- 1   tablespoon olive oil
- ¼   teaspoon salt
- ¼   teaspoon ground cinnamon
- ¼   teaspoon ground coriander
- ¼   teaspoon ground cumin
- 1   garlic clove, minced
- 2   tablespoons chopped fresh cilantro

1. Grate rind from 1 orange with a zester or citrus grater. Remove peel and pith from oranges. Slice each orange into ½-inch-thick round slices; place in a small bowl with zest.

2. Combine olive oil and next 5 ingredients (*olive oil through garlic*) in another small bowl. Pour dressing over oranges and toss gently. Arrange orange slices on salad plates and sprinkle with cilantro. Serves 8.

—Cheryl Forberg

PER SERVING: 140 CALORIES, 6G FAT, 0MG CHOL., 2G PROT., 23G CARBS., 4G FIBER, 150MG SODIUM

Spinach Lasagna

Tomato Sauce

- 3 tablespoons olive oil
- 1 small yellow onion, finely chopped
- 2 garlic cloves, crushed
- 1 (28-ounce) can diced tomatoes, undrained
- 1 (28-ounce) can crushed plum tomatoes, undrained
- 1 tablespoon tomato paste
- 1 teaspoon sugar
- 1 teaspoon kosher salt
- 1 tablespoon dried oregano
- 1 tablespoon dried basil
- ½ teaspoon crushed red pepper
- ½ teaspoon coarsely ground black pepper

Lasagna

- 2 ½ cups whole milk ricotta cheese
- 2 (10-ounce) packages frozen chopped spinach, thawed, drained, and squeezed dry
- 1 egg
- 9 no-cook lasagna noodles
- 1 pound mozzarella cheese, thinly sliced
- ⅔ cup grated Parmigiano-Reggiano cheese

1. To prepare sauce, heat olive oil in a large saucepan. Add onion and garlic; cook until soft and translucent, but not brown.

2. Add tomatoes with their juices, tomato paste, sugar, salt, oregano, basil, crushed red pepper, and pepper; stir well. Bring to a boil. Reduce heat and simmer, uncovered, 30 minutes. Let cool slightly.

3. Preheat oven to 375F.

4. To prepare lasagna, combine ricotta cheese, spinach, and egg in a large bowl; mix well.

5. Coat the bottom of a 13 x 9-inch baking pan with one-third of the tomato sauce. Cover sauce with 3 noodles without overlapping and breaking noodles to fit. Add half of ricotta mixture and half of mozzarella slices. Add half of remaining sauce, 3 noodles, and remaining ricotta mixture and mozzarella. Add remaining noodles, remaining sauce and Parmigiano-Reggiano cheese. (*To make ahead, cover with foil and refrigerate 6 to 8 hours or overnight.*)

6. Place on a baking sheet. Bake, uncovered, 40 minutes, or until bubbling. Add 15 minutes to baking time if lasagna has been refrigerated. Let lasagna sit about 15 minutes before cutting into squares. Serves 12.

—Carolyn Bertagnoli

PER SERVING: 450 CALORIES, 20G FAT, 65MG CHOL., 26G PROT., 43G CARBS., 4G FIBER, 810MG SODIUM

SIMPLE SOLUTION

Place Cards
Apples, pears, oranges, and mini pumpkins make great place card holders. Make a shallow slice into the top of the fruit and insert the card.

SPICED PUMPKIN PIE
A classic that always pleases.

2	eggs
1	unbaked 9-inch pie crust
⅔	cup packed brown sugar
¼	teaspoon salt
1 ½	teaspoons ground cinnamon
1	teaspoon ground ginger
¼	teaspoon ground nutmeg
⅛	teaspoon ground cloves
1	(15-ounce) can pumpkin
1	(12-ounce) can evaporated milk

1. Preheat oven to 350F.
2. Beat eggs in a large bowl. Brush rim of crust with 2 teaspoons beaten egg.
3. Add brown sugar and next 6 ingredients (*brown sugar through pumpkin*); beat with a mixer at medium speed until blended. Gradually beat in milk. Pour into unbaked crust. Bake 40 minutes or until custard is set. Let cool on a wire rack. Serves 8.
—Jean Kressy

PER SERVING: 220 CALORIES, 9G FAT, 70MG CHOL., 7G PROT., 34G CARBS., 3G FIBER, 210MG SODIUM

Holiday Cookie Swap

WANT TO CUT DOWN on holiday baking but still be sure to have sweet treats on hand for the season? Host a cookie swap. Invite several of your friends and ask them to bring two or three varieties of cookies (a few dozen of each). At the party, arrange the cookies on trays, and ask your guests to fill plastic bags or tins that you provide with the cookies and bars they'd like to take home. Trust us, everyone will leave happy.

THE MENU

MANDEL KAKOR (ALMOND COOKIES)
OLD-FASHIONED APPLESAUCE-RAISIN COOKIES
DATE BARS
ALMOND BUTTER–OATMEAL COOKIES
SOUL DOG GLUTEN-FREE CHOCOLATE CHIP COOKIES
GERMAN DROP COOKIES
CHIP-AND-DIP COOKIES

MANDEL KAKOR (ALMOND COOKIES)
Two ounces of almond extract seems like a lot, but we found it to be just right.

- 1 cup unsalted butter, softened
- 1 cup granulated sugar
- 3 cups all-purpose flour
- 1 tablespoon baking powder
- ½ teaspoon salt
- 2 ounces almond extract
- 3 tablespoons heavy cream
- 1 egg, beaten
- Swedish pearl sugar or cake decorating sprinkles

1. Preheat oven to 350F.
2. Combine butter and 1 cup of sugar in a large bowl. Using a mixer at medium-high speed, beat until light. Add flour, baking powder, and salt; beat well. Add almond extract and heavy cream. Mix well.
3. Turn dough out and work into a ball. Cut into 4 portions and refrigerate 10 minutes.
4. Place two portions of dough on a baking sheet. Flatten to ¾ inch thick. Brush tops with beaten egg. Sprinkle pearl sugar on top of each. Repeat with remaining portions of dough on a second baking sheet.
5. Bake 20 minutes. Remove from oven. Increase oven temperature to 300F. Slice each portion into 10 slices and then cut each slice (*except the short ends*) in half. Arrange, cut-side down, on baking sheets. Return to oven and bake 20 minutes for crisp cookies or 10 minutes for chewy cookies. Yield: 70 cookies.
—Erica Schultz

PER (1-COOKIE) SERVING: 50 CALORIES, 3G FAT, 15MG CHOL., 1G PROT., 6G CARBS., 0G FIBER, 40MG SODIUM

OLD-FASHIONED APPLESAUCE-RAISIN COOKIES

¾	cup vegetable shortening
1	cup packed brown sugar
½	cup applesauce
1	egg
2 ½	cups all-purpose flour
½	teaspoon baking soda
½	teaspoon salt
¾	teaspoon ground cinnamon
¼	teaspoon ground cloves
½	cup chopped raisins
½	cup chopped walnuts

1. Preheat oven to 375F.
2. Mix together shortening, brown sugar, applesauce, and egg in a large bowl until smooth. In a separate bowl, combine flour, baking soda, salt, cinnamon, and cloves. Stir flour mixture into applesauce mixture until combined. Drop dough by rounded teaspoons onto two ungreased baking sheets. Top each with walnuts and raisins. Bake 10 to 12 minutes. Let cool on baking sheets 5 minutes before transferring to a wire rack. Yield: 2 dozen.
—Wildflower Inn B & B

PER (1-COOKIE) SERVING: 160 CALORIES, 8G FAT, 10MG CHOL., 2G PROT., 21G CARBS., 1G FIBER, 80MG SODIUM

DATE BARS

Add chopped pecans or walnuts to the crumb mixture if you prefer.

Crumb Mixture

1 ¾	cups quick-cooking oats
1 ¾	cups sifted all-purpose flour
1	cup packed brown sugar
1	teaspoon baking soda
1	cup (2 sticks) butter, softened

Filling

8	ounces chopped dates
½	cup water
1	cup sugar

1. Preheat oven to 350F.

2. To prepare crumb mixture, combine all ingredients and stir until well blended. Press half of mixture into a well-greased 8-inch-square baking dish.

3. To prepare filling, combine all ingredients in a small saucepan; stir well. Cook and stir over medium heat until bubbling and smooth. Pour filling evenly over crumb mixture. Scatter remaining crumb mixture over filling. Bake 25 to 30 minutes, until golden brown. Let cool 10 minutes and cut into squares. Serves 8.

—Mildred Hennon

PER SERVING: 290 CALORIES, 12G FAT, 30MG CHOL., 3G PROT., 46G CARBS., 2G FIBER, 160MG SODIUM

ALMOND BUTTER–OATMEAL COOKIES

10	tablespoons butter, softened
½	cup almond butter
1 ¼	cups granulated sugar
⅔	cup packed brown sugar
2	eggs
1	teaspoon vanilla extract
2 ½	cups quick-cooking oats
1 ½	cups all-purpose flour
1	teaspoon baking soda
1	teaspoon baking powder
¾	teaspoon salt
¾	cup coarsely chopped cashews

1. Preheat oven to 350F.

2. Combine butter and almond butter; beat with mixer at medium speed until light. Add granulated sugar and brown sugar; beat until light and fluffy. Beat in eggs and vanilla.

3. Mix together oats, flour, baking soda, baking powder, and salt in a medium bowl. Stir flour mixture into butter mixture until combined. Stir in cashews. Drop batter by tablespoons onto two baking sheets. Bake 10 to 15 minutes. Yield: 2 dozen.

—Jill Melton

PER (1-COOKIE) SERVING: 210 CALORIES, 11G FAT, 30MG CHOL., 4G PROT., 27G CARBS., 1G FIBER, 240MG SODIUM

SOUL DOG GLUTEN-FREE CHOCOLATE CHIP COOKIES

Soul Dog Bakery in Poughkeepsie, N.Y., substitutes their gluten-free mix cup for cup for wheat flour, except in bread recipes. Look for xanthan gum next to the specialty flours. These are some of the best chocolate chip cookies we've ever had. No one will know (or care) that they're gluten-free.

	Cooking spray
1	cup canola oil
¾	cup granulated sugar
¾	cup brown sugar
2	eggs
1	teaspoon vanilla extract
2 ⅓	cups Gluten-Free Baking Mix
1	teaspoon baking soda
1	teaspoon salt
2	cups semisweet chocolate chips

1. Preheat oven to 350F. Coat a large baking sheet with cooking spray.
2. To prepare cookies, combine oil and sugars in a large bowl; beat with a mixer on medium-high speed. Add eggs, one at a time, mixing until creamy. Add vanilla.
3. Combine Baking Mix, baking soda, and salt in a medium bowl. Gradually add to egg mixture, beating on low speed. Stir in chocolate chips.
5. Drop dough by level tablespoons or a small ice cream scoop 2 inches apart onto a large baking sheet. Flatten slightly.
6. Bake 10 to 12 minutes, or until cookies are golden. Transfer cookies to a wire rack and cool. Yield: about 2 dozen.
—Soul Dog Bakery

PER COOKIE: 250 CALORIES, 15G FAT, 20MG CHOL., 3G PROT., 29G CARBS., 2G FIBER, 250MG SODIUM

GLUTEN-FREE BAKING MIX

2 ⅓	cups chickpea flour
⅔	cup cornstarch
¼	cup sugar
3 ½	teaspoons xanthan gum
1 ½	teaspoons salt
1	teaspoon cream of tartar

Combine all ingredients until evenly blended and store in the refrigerator in an airtight container for up to one month. Makes about 3 ⅓ cups.

GERMAN DROP COOKIES

*These easy cookies are loaded with nuts and
sprinkled with powdered sugar.*

1 ¾	cups all-purpose flour
½	cup granulated sugar
1	cup butter, softened
⅛	teaspoon salt
1	cup chopped pecans
½	cup powdered sugar
½	teaspoon cinnamon

1. Preheat oven to 350F.
2. Combine flour and next 4 ingredients (*flour through
pecans*) in a medium bowl and stir well. Shape dough
into 1-inch balls and place on baking sheets lined with
parchment paper. Bake 20 minutes.
3. Combine powdered sugar and cinnamon. Sift powdered
sugar mixture over warm cookies or roll cookies in sugar
mixture. Yield: 5 dozen.
—Joan Gusweiler

PER (1-COOKIE) SERVING: 60 CALORIES, 4.5G FAT, 10MG CHOL., 1G PROT.,
6G CARBS., 0G FIBER, 25MG SODIUM

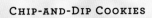

CHIP-AND-DIP COOKIES

CHIP-AND-DIP COOKIES

1	cup (2 sticks) butter, softened
½	cup sugar
1	egg yolk
1	teaspoon vanilla extract
1 ¾	cups all-purpose flour
¾	cup coarsely crushed potato chips
¾	cup coarsely crushed pretzels
1	cup semisweet chocolate chips
1	cup white chocolate chips

1. Preheat oven to 350F.
2. Combine butter and sugar in a large bowl and beat with a mixer at medium-high speed until light and fluffy. Add egg yolk and vanilla. Gradually add flour and mix well. Stir in potato chips and pretzels.
3. Shape level tablespoons of dough into 3-inch logs. Place on an ungreased baking sheet, 1 ½ inches apart. Bake 14 to 18 minutes, until edges are lightly browned. Let cool completely on baking sheet
4. Heat semisweet chocolate chips in microwave for 30 seconds; stir. Repeat until melted. Dip one end of each cookie into melted chocolate and place on wax paper. Refrigerate until firm, about 10 minutes.
5. Heat white chocolate chips in microwave for 30 seconds; stir. Repeat until melted. Dip other end of cookie into melted chocolate and place on wax paper. Refrigerate until firm, about 10 minutes. Yield: 2 dozen.
—Tracy and Danny Schuhmacher

PER (1-COOKIE) SERVING: 240 CALORIES, 15G FAT, 30MG CHOL., 3G PROT., 26G CARBS, 1G FIBER, 150MG SODIUM

SIMPLE SOLUTION

Share the Recipes
Ask your guests to bring copies of the recipes for their cookies. Set the recipes out alongside the cookies.

Christmas Dinner

WHEN MIKE SOLA and Amy-Louise Pfeffer and their daughter, Marta, sit down to Christmas Dinner at Tuckaway Farm in Conway, Massachusetts, they have one fork in Italy and one in America. The dishes are prepared with olive oil from their former grove in Citta della Pieve, Umbria, and the meal ends with steamed cranberry pudding, a New England recipe handed down from Pfeffer's mother.

THE MENU

ROAST PORK LOIN
PARMESAN POTATOES AU GRATIN
GARLICKY BRAISED BROCCOLI RABE
STEAMED CRANBERRY PUDDING WITH BUTTER SAUCE

ROAST PORK LOIN
Apple cider is a simple way to impart both flavor and moisture to our roast pork.

- 1 teaspoon salt
  Coarsely ground black pepper
- 1 (3-pound) boneless pork loin
- 1 long fresh rosemary sprig
- 2 cups apple cider, divided

1. Preheat oven to 350F.
2. Combine salt and pepper; rub evenly onto roast. Make shallow slits over entire surface of roast. Strip rosemary sprig of leaves and insert into slits.
3. Place roast fat-side up in a medium roasting pan. Pour in 1 ½ cups cider. Cook 1 ¼ to 1 ½ hours, basting every 30 minutes, until the internal temperature reaches 155F. Remove from oven and let stand 15 minutes before slicing (*the internal temperature will continue to rise to about 160F*). Add ½ cup cider to pan and place over medium heat. Cook, scraping the bottom of the pan to loosen browned bits. Serve pan drippings with roast. Serves 8.
—Tuckaway Farms

PER SERVING: 250 CALORIES, 7G FAT, 105MG CHOL., 38G PROT., 8G CARBS., 0G FIBER, 380MG SODIUM

WINE PICKS
With the Roast Pork Loin, set out a bottle of red and another of white. For the white, try Chateau Ste. Michelle Pinot Gris (Columbia Valley). It offers a great balance of pear and citrus, creaminess and acidity. MacMurray Ranch Pinot Gris (Sonoma Coast) is a good full-bodied pinot gris with notes of citrus and spice. For the red, try a syrah. It's often served with dishes starring rosemary. Sixth Sense Syrah (Lodi) is a rich, ripe choice for those who like a bold, deeply fruity wine. Most syrahs from Chile offer great value for the price—look for dark fruit flavors with intriguing smoke and violet notes. Favorites include Santa Rita Reserva Shiraz and Arboleda Syrah.

PARMESAN POTATOES AU GRATIN
Yukon gold potatoes get an appealing fragrance from nutmeg and richness from Parmigiano-Reggiano cheese.

- 3 pounds Yukon gold potatoes
- 2 tablespoons butter, divided, plus more for coating the baking dish
- ½ teaspoon kosher salt
  Coarsely ground black pepper

185

1 garlic clove, minced
¼ teaspoon grated nutmeg
¾ cup grated Parmigiano-Reggiano cheese, divided

1. Place potatoes in a large saucepan. Cover with water. Bring to a boil and cook until potatoes are tender, about 15 minutes. Drain. Remove potatoes from the pan to cool. Peel potatoes and cut into pieces. Mash with a potato masher.
2. Add 1 tablespoon of butter, salt, pepper, garlic, nutmeg and ½ cup of cheese to potatoes. Mix well.
3. Preheat broiler. Butter a shallow 2-quart baking dish.
4. Spread potatoes in the prepared baking dish and sprinkle with remaining ¼ cup cheese.
Dot with remaining 1 tablespoon butter.
5. Broil about 6 inches below the broiler element until cheese is golden brown, about 5 minutes. Serves 8.
—Tuckaway Farms

PER SERVING: 200 CALORIES, 5G FAT, 15MG CHOL., 7G PROT., 30G CARBS., 2G FIBER, 270MG SODIUM

GARLICKY BRAISED BROCCOLI RABE
Broccoli rabe is related to both the cabbage and turnip families. The leaves have a pungent, slightly bitter flavor.
Cook broccoli rabe much the same way as you cook broccoli.

2 medium bunches broccoli rabe (about 1 pound), trimmed and coarsely chopped
2 tablespoons extra-virgin olive oil
2 garlic cloves, sliced
½ teaspoon salt
Coarsely ground black pepper

1. Place broccoli rabe in a large saucepan; cover with water. Bring to a boil and cook 2 minutes; drain well.
2. Heat oil in a large skillet over low heat. Add garlic; sauté 3 minutes, taking care not to brown Add broccoli rabe, salt, and pepper; sauté 2 minutes. Serves 8.
—Crescent Dragonwagon

PER SERVING: 70 CALORIES, 5G FAT, 0MG CHOL., 2G PROT., 3G CARBS., 0G FIBER, 160MG SODIUM

PARMESAN POTATOES AU GRATIN

GARLICKY BRAISED BROCCOLI RABE

STEAMED CRANBERRY PUDDING WITH BUTTER SAUCE

The tart flavor of the cranberries cuts through the richness of the butter sauce in this traditional holiday recipe.

Pudding

	Butter
1 ½	cups fresh cranberries
1	egg
1	tablespoon sugar
½	cup light molasses (not blackstrap)
2	teaspoons baking soda
⅓	cup hot water
1 ½	cups all-purpose flour
½	teaspoon kosher salt

Butter Sauce

2	cups sugar
1	cup (2 sticks) butter
1	cup heavy or whipping cream
2	teaspoons vanilla extract

1. To prepare pudding, butter a 6-cup soufflé dish. Select a large pot with a lid that will hold the soufflé dish and several inches of water.

2. Place cranberries in a medium saucepan. Cover with water. Cover and cook over medium heat until cranberries begin to pop and water is absorbed, about 15 minutes.

3. Beat together egg, sugar, and molasses in a large bowl until combined. Mix together baking soda and hot water until baking soda dissolves. Add to egg mixture. Combine flour and salt in a small bowl; add to egg mixture, stirring just until blended. Do not over mix. Stir in cranberries.

4. Pour batter into prepared dish. Cover tightly with foil. Place dish in the large pot. Add enough water to come halfway up the side of the dish. Cover the pot and bring water to a boil. Reduce heat and simmer 70 to 90 minutes until pudding is firm. Run a paring knife around the edge of the pudding to loosen and unmold onto a serving platter.

5. To prepare sauce, combine all ingredients in a saucepan. Cook over low heat until thickened, about 30 minutes, stirring occasionally. Place warm sauce in a bowl or pitcher to pass with the pudding at the table. Serves 10.

—Tuckaway Farms

PER SERVING: 470 CALORIES, 28G FAT, 105G CHOL., 3G PROT., 58G CARBS., 1G FIBER, 500MG SODIUM

SIMPLE SOLUTION

Votives
Keep a large bag of votive candles on hand, and place them in small glasses. Place star anise or cardamon pods in between candle and glass.

STEAMED CRANBERRY PUDDING
WITH BUTTER SAUCE

Holiday Breakfast

DURING THE HOLIDAYS, people all over the world celebrate by baking bread. Not your everyday sandwich loaf, but breads rich with ingredients that signify this special time of year: spices and liqueurs that only occasionally leave their place in the pantry; larger-than-usual quantities of butter and eggs; and nuts and dried fruits. Yeast-risen, whether braided and folded or sugared and glazed, holiday breads entice passersby from bakery windows in Italy, France, Germany, Hungary, Czechoslovakia, and everywhere in between. And in many homes in those countries, you may find panettone or stollen rising in a warm corner or scenting the air as it bakes, with aromas that say "home for the holidays" in a visceral way. Here is a holiday breakfast anchored by two festive holiday breads, but because guests can't live by bread alone, there are eggs and a salmon dish too.

—*Crescent Dragonwagon*

THE MENU

PANETTONE QUICK BREAD
STOLLEN
BAKED EGGS WITH MUSHROOMS **or**
SMOKED SALMON KEDGEREE

PANETTONE QUICK BREAD

Traditional panettone, a sweet bread with its roots in Milan, Italy, is a delectable but incredibly complex-to-make affair involving sourdough, proofing, and curing. We've created a buttery quick bread with the traditional golden raisins, pine nuts, and an optional anise glaze. If you can't find anise extract, double or triple the amount of anise seeds.

	Cooking spray
1	egg
2	egg yolks
1	cup sugar
½	cup (1 stick) butter, melted and cooled to room temperature
1	teaspoon anise extract
3	cups sifted all-purpose flour
2	teaspoons baking powder
½	teaspoon salt
1	cup 2% reduced-fat milk
½	cup pine nuts, lightly toasted
½	cup golden raisins
2	teaspoons finely grated lemon rind
1	teaspoon anise seeds
	Anise Glaze (optional) (recipe on page 193)

1. Preheat oven to 350F. Coat two 9 x 5-inch standard or decorative loaf pans with cooking spray.
2. Beat egg, yolks, and sugar with a mixer on medium speed until thick and pale yellow. Beat in butter and anise extract.
3. Sift together flour, baking powder, and salt. Stir half of flour mixture into butter mixture with a wooden spoon. Stir in milk and remaining flour alternately. Stir in raisins, lemon rind, and anise seeds just until evenly distributed.
4. Divide batter evenly between prepared pans. Bake about 25 to 30 minutes, until golden brown and fragrant. Let breads cool in pans 10 minutes on a wire rack. Remove from pans and let cool completely on the rack. When cool, ice with Anise Glaze, if using. Serves 16.

—Crescent Dragonwagon

PER SERVING (WITH GLAZE): 280 CALORIES, 10G FAT, 55MG CHOL., 4G PROT., 46G CARBS., 1G FIBER, 200MG SODIUM

BAKED EGGS WITH MUSHROOMS

2	tablespoons butter
1	cup chopped white mushrooms
⅓	cup chopped onion
3	tablespoons chopped cooked ham
½	cup lower-sodium beef broth
⅛	teaspoon coarsely ground black pepper
4	eggs, at room temperature
¼ to ½	cup shredded Cheddar or Swiss cheese

1. Preheat oven to 350F.

2. Melt butter in a medium skillet over medium heat. Stir in mushrooms and onions; sauté 2 minutes. Stir in ham; sauté 2 minutes. Add broth; cook 3 minutes. Add pepper .

3. Divide mixture among 4 well-buttered ramekins. Break 1 egg into each. Bake 15 minutes. Sprinkle cheese on top; cook 5 minutes more, or until eggs are set. Serves 4.

—Elaine Morehead

PER SERVING: 170 CALORIES, 14G FAT, 240MG CHOL., 1G PROT., 3G CARBS., 0G FIBER, 250MG SODIUM

ANISE GLAZE FOR PANETTONE QUICK BREAD

If you have anisette or sambuca liqueur on hand, use it instead of water and omit the anise extract.

2	cups powdered sugar, sifted
2 to 3	tablespoons water or lemon juice
1	teaspoon anise extract

Combine all ingredients, mixing until smooth, adding the liquid gradually until glaze is the consistency of heavy cream. Pour or spoon the glaze over the panettones, allowing it drip down the sides.

STOLLEN

Stollen was born in Dresden, Germany, as long ago as the Middle Ages. With shortcuts and do-ahead options, we've brought this ancient bread into the present. What we have kept is the distinctive cardamom flavor from whole cardamom seeds and a luxurious browned-butter topping. One bite and you'll kiss fruitcake good-bye forever: this is the ultimate holiday treat.

Stollens

8	pods cardamom
1	cup 2% reduced-fat milk, scalded
½	cup golden raisins
1	cup dried cherries
3	tablespoons dark rum or orange juice
2	(.25-ounce) packages active dry yeast
¼	cup warm water
⅓	cup sugar, divided
3 ½	cups all-purpose flour, divided
½	cup (1 stick) cold butter, cut into 8 pieces
½	teaspoon salt
1	tablespoon finely grated lemon rind
1	egg
2	egg yolks
½	cup slivered almonds, toasted
10	ounces almond paste

Topping

½	cup (1 stick) salted butter
1	cup powdered sugar

1. To prepare stollens, place cardamom pods in a small bowl. Add hot milk. Let stand 10 minutes.

2. Combine raisins and cherries with rum. Let stand.

3. Combine yeast, warm water, and 1 teaspoon sugar. Set aside to soften and foam, about 10 minutes.

4. Remove cardamom pods from milk. Squeeze pods open. Scrape small black seeds into milk. Discard pods. Stir milk into yeast mixture. Add 1 cup of flour; beat well. Cover this mixture (*called the "sponge"*) with plastic wrap; let rise 30 minutes.

5. As the sponge rises, place 2 cups flour and butter pieces in a food processor. Add salt and remaining sugar. Pulse 6 or 8 times.

6. Drain fruits, reserving soaking liquid. When the sponge is ready, add it to the processor, along with lemon rind, egg, and egg yolks, and soaking liquid from dried fruits. Process 20 or 30 seconds, until dough is thoroughly mixed. Then, with a few quick pulses, add fruits, almonds, and remaining ½ cup flour. Scrape dough, which will be quite tender, into a bowl, and refrigerate overnight.

7. In the morning, punch dough down, and divide into thirds. On a floured board, gently pull and pat each portion of dough into an oval, about 14 inches long by 10 inches wide. Divide almond paste into thirds. Patting with your hands, cover half of each oval, the long way, with bits of almond paste (*don't worry about covering it neatly*). Fold the other half of the dough over it, gently enclosing the almond paste and making a pastry that is a plump half-moon.

8. Carefully transfer to 2 or 3 parchment-lined baking sheets Let rise until dough is puffy, though not quite doubled in bulk, about 1 hour.

9. Preheat oven to 350F.

10. Bake 25 minutes, or until a golden brown.

11. To prepare topping, place ½ cup butter in a small saucepan over medium heat. When butter melts, lower heat and let butter cook until browned and fragrant, about 8 minutes. Watch carefully and shake the pan if needed.

12. Using 2 spatulas, transfer stollens to wire racks; let cool about 10 minutes, then spoon browned butter over the tops. Sift powdered sugar generously over tops. Let cool at least 20 minutes, until sugar sets slightly. Serve, in thin slices, slightly warm or at room temperature. Yield: 3 stollens (*8 servings each*).

Note: The stollens can be stored, wrapped in plastic, in the freezer, for up to one month.

—Crescent Dragonwagon

PER SERVING: 220 CALORIES, 10G FAT, 36MG CHOL., 4G PROT., 22G CARBS., 1.5G FIBER, 92MG SODIUM

SMOKED SALMON KEDGEREE

Kedgeree is a popular English breakfast dish consisting of rice, hard-cooked eggs, and salmon. Be sure to use hot-smoked salmon rather than cold-smoked (lox).

2	cups water
2	cups bottled clam juice
2	cups long-grain white rice
1	tablespoon curry powder
¼	cup vegetable oil
1	onion, chopped
½	cup frozen green peas, thawed
½	cup fresh or frozen corn kernels
4	hard-cooked eggs, chopped
10	ounces hot-smoked salmon, broken into chunks
¼	cup chopped flat-leaf parsley (optional)

1. Bring water and clam juice to a boil; add rice and curry powder. Cover, reduce heat, and simmer 15 to 20 minutes until liquid is absorbed.

2. Heat oil in a large skillet over medium heat. Add onion and sauté until golden, about 10 minutes. Stir in rice and sauté 1 minute. Stir in peas and corn; cook 2 minutes. Stir in eggs and salmon; toss to combine and cook over low heat until thoroughly heated. Garnish with parsley. Serves 6.

—Martin Booe

PER SERVING: 420 CALORIES, 15G FAT, 155MG CHOL., 19G PROT., 53G CARBS., 2G FIBER, 600MG SODIUM

SIMPLE SOLUTION

Storing Leftover Wine

Oxidation is the culprit responsible for handing opened wine a one-way ticket to a bitter destination: vinegar. The easiest way to slow down oxidation is to simply shove the cork back in and stick the wine in the fridge. But refrigerating alone isn't failsafe, and it works far better for white wines than it does for high-quality reds. A better route is to minimize wine's contact with the villain—oxygen. One way to do this is by transferring leftover wine to a smaller container—preferably one just big enough to accommodate the leftovers. Empty half-size (375ml) wine bottles often are perfect for this.

Or, you can eliminate oxygen-wine contact with one of several available products. One type utilizes a special stopper and pump to vacuum oxygen from the bottle. Another consists of a gas sprayed into the bottle to form a barrier between wine and oxygen.

Christmas/Hanukkah Dinner Party

THE COUNTRY'S ESTIMATED one million interfaith families have twice as much to celebrate during the holiday season. Interfaith holidays are all about warm gatherings of friends and family—and sharing great food from different traditions. Our menu acknowledges customary flavors from both Christmas and Hanukkah at one table with beef tenderloin, crisp latkes, and an apple-onion relish in the Eastern European Jewish tradition. Everyone at the table will agree—it's heavenly.

THE MENU

PROSECCO SUNRISE PUNCH
GARLIC AND HERB BEEF TENDERLOIN
APPLE-ONION RELISH
POTATO LATKES

PROSECCO SUNRISE PUNCH

What better way to start a holiday brunch than with this very grown-up, easy-to-drink sparkling punch. The beautiful color—orange tinged with red—seems to make the table come alive. Just think, all that and vitamin C too!

1	(750ml) bottle Prosecco, chilled
3 ¼	cups orange juice, chilled
2	cups orange-flavored seltzer water, chilled
½	cup Triple Sec
12	teaspoons grenadine
6	orange slices, cut into halves

Combine Prosecco, orange juice, seltzer, and Triple Sec in a large bowl. Ladle into 12 champagne flutes or wine glasses. Slowly pour 1 teaspoon of grenadine into each. Garnish rim of glasses with an orange slice. Serves 12.
—Marge Perry and David Bonom

PER SERVING: 130 CALORIES, 0G FAT, 0MG CHOL., 1G PROT., 22G CARBS., 0G FIBER, 10MG SODIUM

GARLIC AND HERB BEEF TENDERLOIN

1	cup packed fresh basil
3	tablespoons fresh rosemary
3	tablespoons fresh marjoram
2	tablespoons fresh oregano
6	garlic cloves
3	tablespoons Dijon mustard
¼	teaspoon coarsely ground black pepper
⅓	cup olive oil
1	(4 ¼ pound) beef tenderloin, trimmed and tied
	Cooking Spray
1 ½	teaspoons salt

1. Combine basil and next 6 ingredients (*basil through pepper*) in a food processor or blender. With the food processor running, slowly drizzle in oil and process until herbs and garlic are very finely chopped. Rub herb mixture over beef, transfer to a large plate, cover loosely with plastic wrap, and refrigerate at least 4 hours and up to 24 hours.

PROSECCO SUNRISE PUNCH

GARLIC AND HERB BEEF TENDERLOIN

197

2. Preheat oven to 425F. Coat a rimmed baking sheet with cooking spray.
3. Transfer beef to baking sheet. Sprinkle with salt. Bake 25 to 30 minutes, until a thermometer inserted into the center registers 135F for medium-rare. Remove from oven and let stand 10 minutes before slicing. Serves 12.
—Marge Perry and David Bonom

PER SERVING: 230 CALORIES, 12G FAT, 85MG CHOL., 31G PROT., 1G CARBS., 0G FIBER, 420MG SODIUM

APPLE-ONION RELISH

A spiced fruit relish brimming with flavors is lighter than béarnaise or other butter-based sauces that are typically served with beef tenderloin

2	tablespoons vegetable oil
3	onions, chopped
3	garlic cloves, minced
½	cup sugar
⅓	cup cider vinegar
½	teaspoon ground cumin
¼	teaspoon ground ginger
¼	teaspoon ground cinnamon
2	Golden Delicious apples, peeled, cored, and diced
1	cup golden raisins
2	tablespoons apple jelly
¼	teaspoon salt

1. Heat oil in a large nonstick skillet. Add onions, garlic, and sugar; cook, stirring occasionally, until caramelized, about 35 minutes. Stir in vinegar, cumin, ginger, and cinnamon; cook 7 minutes. Add apples and raisins; cook 5 minutes.
2. Remove from heat and stir in jelly and salt. Serve warm or at room temperature. Serves 12.
—Marge Perry and David Bonom

PER SERVING: 130 CALORIES, 2G FAT, 0MG CHOL., 1G PROT., 27G CARBS., 2G FIBER, 55MG SODIUM.

POTATO LATKES

2	pounds russet potatoes, peeled and shredded
2	onions, shredded (about 1 ½ cups)
⅓	cup all-purpose flour
2	eggs
½	teaspoon dried thyme
1 ¼	teaspoons salt
¼	teaspoon coarsely ground black pepper
¼	cup vegetable oil
¼	cup olive oil

1. Place shredded potatoes in a colander. Press to squeeze out liquid.
2. Combine potato, onion, flour, eggs, thyme, salt, and pepper; mix well.
3. Pour half of vegetable oil and half of olive oil into a large nonstick skillet; heat until hot but not smoking. Spoon 2 tablespoons potato mixture per latke into the skillet, spreading into 3-inch rounds with a fork. Cook until brown on both sides, about 3 to 5 minutes on each side. Drain on paper towels and sprinkle with additional salt. Repeat with remaining potato mixture, adding oil to the skillet as needed. Serve immediately. Yield: 24 latkes.
—Marge Perry and David Bonom

PER (1-LATKE) SERVING: 90 CALORIES, 5G FAT, 20MG CHOL., 2G PROT., 9G CARBS., 1G FIBER, 150MG SODIUM.

New Year's Eve Communal Lobster Pot

OFFER A BETTER OPTION to friends reluctant to brave the December 31st fray: lobster at home among your nearest and dearest. Prepare a large stockpot filled with lemons, white wine, herbs, and spices. Guests bring champagne and their own lobster tails, ready to take the savory plunge. Start with a first course of linguine with arugula and shallots, then move at your own pace to a grapefruit and avocado salad. The highlight is the lobster feast. Pots de crème provide a chocolate pick-me-up late in the evening to prepare guests for toasting the New Year, relaxed, well-fed, and in good company.

THE MENU

WHOLE-WHEAT LINGUINE WITH ARUGULA AND SHALLOTS

RUBY RED GRAPEFRUIT AND AVOCADO SALAD WITH CITRUS-CHAMPAGNE VINAIGRETTE

LOBSTER TAILS WITH SPICY LEMON BUTTER

CHOCOLATE POTS DE CRÈME

WHOLE-WHEAT LINGUINE WITH ARUGULA AND SHALLOTS

Use a sweeter bread for the bread bits.

4	tablespoons extra-virgin olive oil
1	tablespoon sugar
2	cups diced shallots
1	teaspoon sea salt
½	teaspoon coarsely ground black pepper
½	teaspoon crushed red pepper
1	pound whole wheat linguine
10	ounces arugula, washed, spun dry, and stemmed if needed
1	bunch Italian flat-leaf parsley, coarsely chopped
2	cups toasted bread bits (from a crusty loaf), cut like baby croutons
½	pound Pecorino Sardo or Romano cheese, grated

1. Heat oil in a large skillet. Add sugar and shallots, cook until caramelized, 10 to 15 minutes. Add salt, pepper, and crushed red pepper.
2. Bring 6 quarts of lightly salted water to a boil in a stockpot. Add linguine and cook until al dente, about 10 minutes. Drain, reserving 1 cup cooking water, and return to pot. Scrape shallots and oil into pot; toss until linguine is well coated.
3. At serving time, gently warm linguine and fold in arugula, parsley, and a little reserved cooking water. (*The heat will wilt these greens.*) Add toasted bread bits and cheese, folding until evenly distributed throughout the pasta. Add more salt and pepper if needed. Serves 8.
—Nancy Vienneau

PER SERVING: 440 CALORIES, 16G FAT, 20MG CHOL., 19G PROT., 53G CARBS., 10G FIBER, 830MG SODIUM

WINE PICKS:
As a hostess gift or for kicking off holiday gatherings with style, bubblies simply can't be beat. And what would New Year's Eve be without a little sparkle? True French Champagne can be over-the-moon expensive; when you're ready for a splurge, try Tattinger La Française (Champagne, France) or Perrier Jouët Grand Brut (Champagne, France). French winemakers outside of the Champagne region possess plenty of savoir-faire when it comes to bubbles, and their products are often great values. Try Pierre Spar Marquis de Perlade (Alsace, France) or Bouvet Signature Brut (Saumur, France). Combining California fruit with French panache, try Mumm Napa Blanc de Noirs, Domaine Carneros Brut by Taittinger, or Roederer Estate Anderson Valley Brut for great values stateside.

For inexpensive sparkling wines, try Cristalino Brut Cava (Spain); François Montand Blanc de Blanc (France); Mumm Cuvée M (Napa Valley); and Roederer Estate Brut (Anderson Valley, California). For higher end bubblies, look for creamy, crisp and elegant Schramsberg Blanc de Noirs 2006 or Louis Roederer Brut Premier Champagne.

WHOLE-WHEAT LINGUINE
WITH ARUGULA AND SHALLOTS

Ruby Red Grapefruit and Avocado Salad with Citrus-Champagne Vinaigrette

Vinaigrette
- 2 tablespoons champagne vinegar
- 2 tablespoons grapefruit juice
- 1 tablespoon chopped chives
- 1 teaspoon grated lime rind
- ½ teaspoon coarsely ground black pepper
- ¼ teaspoon dry mustard
- Pinch salt
- ½ cup walnut oil

Salad
- 2 avocados, peeled, pitted, and thinly sliced
- Juice of 1 lime
- 1 large head butter lettuce, separated into leaves
- 2 ruby red grapefruit, peeled and sectioned (reserve juice for dressing)
- ½ red onion, slivered
- ½ cup chopped walnuts, toasted

1. To prepare vinaigrette, place all ingredients except oil in food processor. Process while adding walnut oil 1 tablespoon at a time.
2. To prepare salad, sprinkle avocado slices with lime juice.
3. Place butter lettuce leaves onto 8 salad plates. Compose salad with grapefruit, avocado, and onion. Top with toasted walnuts. Drizzle with about half the vinaigrette and serve. Serves 8.
—Nancy Vienneau

PER SERVING: 220 CALORIES, 19G FAT, 0MG CHOL., 3G PROT., 14G CARBS., 7G FIBER, 5MG SODIUM.

Lobster Tails

- 12 cups water
- 4 cups white wine
- 2 lemons, cut into halves
- 2 to 3 celery stalks with leaves, chopped
- 1 large onion, quartered
- 4 to 5 garlic cloves
- 2 to 3 bay leaves
- 1 tablespoon hot pepper sauce
- 2 teaspoons sea salt
- 1 teaspoon celery seed
- 1 teaspoon mustard seed
- ½ teaspoon crushed red pepper
- Several thyme sprigs
- 12 to 16 lobster tails

1. Place all ingredients, except lobster, in a large stockpot. Cover and simmer until onion is tender, about 45 minutes.
2. Prepare lobster tails for cooking by using kitchen shears to cut up the center of the underside of the tail. Cut off swimmerets. Gently flex the base of the tail backward until it cracks; this action makes it easier to remove meat after poaching. Rinse well.
3. Plunge the tails into the gently boiling liquid. Cook for 5 to 7 minutes. Turn off the heat. Tails can stay in the liquid until serving time. Serves 8.
—Nancy Vienneau

PER (8-OUNCE) SERVING: 220 CALORIES, 1.5 G. FAT, 160MG CHOL., 46G PROT., 3G CARBS., 0G FIBER, 860MG SODIUM

201

SPICY LEMON BUTTER

8	tablespoons (1 stick) unsalted butter
3	tablespoons freshly squeezed lemon juice
1	tablespoon hot pepper sauce
⅛	teaspoon cayenne pepper
⅛	teaspoon sea salt

Melt butter in a small saucepan over low heat. Stir in juice, hot sauce, pepper, and salt. Divide among individual dipping bowls. Serves 8.

—Nancy Vienneau

PER SERVING: 100 CALORIES, 12G FAT, 30MG CHOL., 0G PROT., 1G CARBS., 0G FIBER, 80MG SODIUM.

CHOCOLATE POTS DE CRÈME

8	ounces semisweet chocolate
1 ½	cups heavy cream
1	cup 2% reduced-fat milk
1	tablespoon strong brewed coffee
2	teaspoons vanilla extract
6	egg yolks
1	tablespoon sugar
$1/16$	teaspoon salt
	Unsweetened whipped cream (optional)
	Small strawberries (optional)

1. Preheat oven to 300 degrees.

2. Chop chocolate finely and place in a bowl.

3. Heat cream, milk, coffee, and vanilla in a saucepan over medium-high heat until bubbles form around the edge (*do not boil*). Pour over chocolate. Whisk until all chocolate melts and mixture is well blended.

4. Beat egg yolks with sugar and salt.

5. Add 1 cup chocolate mixture to egg mixture, whisking to blend thoroughly. Add this back to the remaining chocolate mixture; whisk until well blended.

6. Divide among 8 ramekins. Cover ramekins tightly with foil and place in baking dish. Pour in enough water to come halfway up the sides of ramekins. Bake 30 to 40 minutes.

7. Uncover and let cool. Chill 5 hours.

8. Serve with unsweetened whipped cream and fresh strawberries, if desired. Serves 8.

—Nancy Vienneau

PER SERVING: 360 CALORIES, 29G FAT, 220MG CHOL., 6G PROT., 23G CARBS., 0G FIBER, 75MG SODIUM.

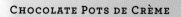

CHOCOLATE POTS DE CRÈME

203

CONTRIBUTORS

NANCY KRECK ALLEN
RELISH CHEF JON ASHTON
CHEF MICHELLE BERNSTEIN,
   MICHY'S AND SRA. MARTINEZ
   (MIAMI, FLORIDA)
CAROLYN BERTAGNOLI
MONICA BHIDE
TERESA BLACKBURN
ROSELL BOCCHIERI
DAVID BONOM
MARTIN BOOE
PETER BRONSKI
CLAUDIA CARAUNA
CHEF JEFF CARTER,
   DANCING BEAR LODGE
   (TOWNSEND, TENNESSEE)
TRACEY CEURVELS
CHERRY MARKETING INSTITUTE
CHARMIAN CHRISTIE
CHEF TED CIZMA
HOLLY CLEGG
LYNN SAMPSON CURRY
LAUREN BANK DEEN
CHEF PAULA DISBROWE,
   HART & HOUND FITNESS RANCH
   (RIO FRIO, TEXAS)
CRESCENT DRAGONWAGON
SYDNEY AND ROGER DROTAR
CHRISTINA ENG
FLAG HILL FARM
   (VERSHIRE, VERMONT)
CANDACE FLOYD
CHERYL FORBERG
DAMON LEE FOWLER
KRISTINE GASBARRE
ROZANNE GOLD
CHEF JESUS GONZALEZ,
   RANCHO LA PUERTA SPA
   (TECATE, MEXICO)
PATRICIA GRIFFITH,
   SOUTHERN OVEN FOODS
   (LOS ANGELES)

JOAN GUSWEILER
SANDRA GUTIERREZ
TAMAR HASPEL
MILDRED HENNON
JULIE HESSION
LISA HOLDERNESS
CHEF DOUG HOSFORD
JEANNETTE HURT
MORGAN JARRETT
JEAN KRESSY
MARY J. LEWIS
JO MARSHALL
JILL MELTON
WINI MORANVILLE
ELAINE MOREHEAD
MOTHER'S BISTRO
   (PORTLAND, OREGON)
VINCENT NATTRESS
   (NAPA VALLEY
   MUSTARD FESTIVAL)
ROBIN NOELLE
GREG PATENT
PEARSON FARM
   (FORT VALLEY, GEORGIA)
LARAINE PERRI
MARGE PERRY
CHEF MICHAEL PSILAKIS,
   ANTHOS (NEW YORK)
GRETCHEN ROBERTS
KORY ROLLISON
MICHAELA ROSENTHAL
MERCEDES SANCHEZ
MARK SCARBROUGH
TRACY AND DANNY SCHUHMACHER
ERICA SCHULTZ
LIZ SHENK
DONNA SHIELDS
LAUREN SHOCKEY
SOUL DOG BAKERY
   (POUGHKEEPSIE, NEW YORK)
TUCKAWAY FARMS
   (CONWAY, MASSACHUSETTS)
BRUCE WEINSTEIN
WILDFLOWER INN B & B
   (LYNDONVILLE, VERMONT)
NANCY VIENNEAU